AMERICA
FARM TO TABLE

AMERICA
FARM TO TABLE

SIMPLE, DELICIOUS RECIPES CELEBRATING LOCAL FARMERS

MARIO BATALI
AND JIM WEBSTER

ART DIRECTION BY Douglas Riccardi

RECIPE PHOTOGRAPHY BY Quentin Bacon

FARM PHOTOGRAPHY BY Christine Birch Ferrelli AND Lara Cerri

GRAND CENTRAL
L&S
LIFE & STYLE
NEWYORK · BOSTON

Grand Central Life & Style
Hachette Book Group
1290 Avenue of the Americas
New York, NY 10019
GrandCentralLifeandStyle.com

Designed by Memo, NY

Printed in the United States of America

WOR

First Edition: October 2014
10 9 8 7 6 5 4 3 2 1

Grand Central Life & Style is an imprint of Grand Central Publishing.
The Grand Central Life & Style name and logo are trademarks of
Hachette Book Group, Inc.

The Hachette Speakers Bureau provides a wide range of authors for speaking
events. To find out more, go to www.HachetteSpeakersBureau.com or call
(866) 376-6591.

The publisher is not responsible for websites (or their content) that are not
owned by the publisher.

Library of Congress Cataloging-in-Publication Data
Batali, Mario.
   America—farm to table : simple, delicious recipes celebrating local
farmers / Mario Batali and Jim Webster ; recipe photography by Quentin
Bacon ; farm photography by Christine Birch Ferrelli and Lara Cerri.
      pages cm
   Includes index.
      ISBN 978-1-4555-8468-0 (hc) — ISBN 978-1-4555-8469-7 (ebook)
1. Cooking, American.   2. Local foods—United States.   3. Farms,
small—United States.   I. Webster, Jim.   II. Title.
   TX715.B34358 2014
   641.5973—dc23
                                          2014011984
ISBN 978-1-4555-8974-6 (signed edition hc)

To my wife and farmer, Susi Cahn,
and our two boys, Benno and Leo,
who love time on any farm

And to everyone who farms or gardens for their pleasure,
nourishment, or mental calm

Contents

FARMERS ARE THE REAL ROCK STARS

In the last decade, the concept of "farm-to-table" has become an obsession in the media, in restaurants, in foodie magazines, and in television programming.

Although slogans are among my least favorite ways to communicate, I believe that the fundamental truth of supporting local small farming may in fact be a panacea for many of our twenty-first-century problems in both nutrition and regional economic development. But it is also crucial in our hedonistic search for the delicious and the delightful in cooking at home.

I grew up in Washington state in the sixties and seventies, when rural small farms supported and were supported by small communities on both sides of the Cascades. Before it was considered special or sacred, and long before the Food Network and *Iron Chef*, and even before Alice Waters and Jeremiah Tower, families in our community went shopping in the lower valley farmers' markets—right there on the actual farms in the lower valley itself—for vegetables and fruits to pickle, preserve, marinate, can, jar, turn into pies and jams, and just plain eat—cooked or raw—in simple tribute to true seasonality and the magnificence of inexpensive freshness. It was not considered a luxury to drive an hour or two to get six cases of tomatoes, fragrant with the sticky-sweet, piney, acrid, dusty, chalky, sharp, sensational, "geranium high on margaritas" scent of the tomato vines I associate with the ecstasy of childhood. In our family, it was simply what we did.

Since the mid-1960s, the United States' obsession with processed foods has increased from just a hobby or a special-occasion treat to a daily first choice for many of our meals, which in itself can explain a lot about our decline in national health. Type 2 diabetes diagnoses have quickly ascended to alarming and potentially catastrophic numbers,

putting an even higher priority on the dietary habits and health of children. The reduction of actual dietary fiber in processing leaves all of us capable of consuming much more food than we need, and the lack of plant-based fiber is most certainly a major culprit in heart disease and diabetes.

Not all of the decline in vigor and health is based on where we live or what we eat, but certainly nutrition is a big part of our health problems and, to me, seems the area easiest to improve upon. What yields the most delicious, healthful results is, in fact, the simplest: cooking at home.

In the last twenty years or so, professional cooks and chefs have ascended the social ladder from the outcasts and bottom rung-ers wearing grungy T-shirts and dirty aprons catching a smoke by the alley Dumpster to a near rock-star status. This phenomenon is due in part to the increased realization of the importance of food as fuel for health, but also in part to the entertainment component of watching chefs on TV and the pleasure of going out to a restaurant for dinner. It used to be that a group of friends would head to the game and get a bite, or go to the theater and catch a bite after. In short, the "bite" part, in my mom and dad's time, was usually perceived as an adjunct to the main event. In the 1980s, chefs emerged from the back of the house and became entertainers themselves, and have remained on center stage ever since. I believe this change is related to the fact that the meal in itself—the traditions, the provocation, the innovation, and the execution—have now become as appreciated as a fine performance on a theatrical stage, or even an excellent game on a sporting field. Chefs became the rock stars, the lead players, or the quarterbacks of the increasingly significant nightly performances onstage at great restaurants around the world.

Cooking shows have thrived and given rise to hundreds of offshoots and derivatives. And, although I am not a big fan of competition reality programming, excellent cooking advice and lifestyle shows are constantly upping the ante, introducing the next food-porn star. Many home cooks in the country live vicariously through such food television, and may never intend to replicate the *Iron Chef* dishes at home. But there is also a huge contingent of viewers, fans, and followers intent on improving their own cooking at home, wanting to create restaurant-style food in their own kitchens. They buy sous-vide technology, immerse themselves in cookbooks by renowned and justly celebrated technicians such as Thomas Keller and Grant Achatz, and lust for every delicious tip, whispering each trade secret conspiratorially, sotto voce, in anticipation of cracking the code to create the perfect dish. The good news is that the specialty equipment we use in our professional kitchens can now be purchased by consumers on the open market. The bad news is that we have incredible human resources in our talented chefs and cooks in numbers that the home kitchen could never support.

The single most important trick to elevating the home cook's potential to create quality, restaurant-level food is much simpler: It is the sourcing of quality ingredients. Such ingredients yield better results than buying the oven or immersion circulator I use. Instead, buy the same tiny waxy golden potatoes, or the rainbow chard, or the real farm-fresh eggs, or the exact baby arugula borne of seeds carried by hand from the shadow of Vesuvius and grown by a farmer I know and love.

The real story here is that the farmers from whom chefs buy produce and meat are capable of changing the food you eat at home much more significantly than equipment or cookbooks or tips or TV shows you watch. This creates the new paradigm: Where chefs once ruled the waves, local small farmers are the new rock stars.

I would like to introduce you to an old pal of mine, and the coauthor of this book, Jim Webster. Jim is a journalist by training and was working at the *St. Petersburg Times* when I met him, but he now works at the *Washington Post* as a multiplatform editor (huh?). In any case, Jim and I share similar passions about food, and we both have particular interest in where it comes from. We hatched the idea that the real story in the twenty-first century is the tale of where and how the raw ingredients are born; and the real action surrounds the artist or farmer who makes the food happen. Jim and I identified fourteen of my favorite chefs around the country and asked each of them to identify a farmer/forager/producer he or she strongly believed in. That was the easy part.

Jim traveled the country to meet both the chefs and the farmers, and discovered that both groups are incredibly busy, and although they had agreed on paper to participate in this book idea, they had very little real time to hang out with Jim and chitchat…They are, in fact, always working hard at weaving the fabric of deliciousness that makes them interesting. But Jim persevered, and the results of that dedication are the fascinating stories of the farmers and their farms and the products they curate, as well as the eventual delivery of those quality products to a plate on the table.

After hearing about and tasting the great products of these farmers, I was inspired to create recipes that featured them in all their glory, and that is what you'll find on the following pages. These are not the actual recipes gleaned from a restaurant or a television show, but are instead a loose itinerary, or road map, that will hopefully lead you to develop relationships with local farmers, as well as to the improvisational style of cooking that will elevate the flavor of the dishes you create in your own kitchen when you buy products from a farm or at a farmers' market and bring them directly to your table.

In the final analysis, "farm-to-table" transcends slogans when the farmer and the cook exchange not only commerce in the form of trade, but also joy and passion for food, health, and love of life in the form of real communication. The human touch is the single most significant and magnificent component of this process, and to eschew the machine-made and the mass-produced in favor of handmade is the very best recipe of all.

One:
APPETIZERS

CARROT FRITTELLE

with Feta Cheese

MAKES 32 TO 36 FRITTELLE

5 large carrots

Kosher salt and freshly ground black pepper

4 large eggs, beaten

½ cup panko bread crumbs

¼ cup rye flour

3 tablespoons grated caciotta or Pecorino Romano

¼ cup extra-virgin olive oil

8 ounces goat's milk feta or regular feta, coarsely grated

1 lemon, cut into wedges

This is a traditional antipasto all over northern Italy, where they will substitute any firm vegetable for the carrots depending on the season. I love the Texas-based Mozzarella Company cheeses, and here I recommend using two of them, the caciotta and the goat's milk feta, but you could substitute local cheeses from wherever you like.

Shred the carrots in your food processor using the finest grating disk, or on the finest holes of a box grater. Place the shredded carrots in a large bowl and season with salt and pepper. Add the eggs, panko, rye flour, and caciotta and stir to combine.

In a 10- to 12-inch nonstick sauté pan, heat the oil. Add the carrot mixture, 1 tablespoon at a time, and cook until each fritter is golden brown on both sides. Transfer the fritters to a serving platter and repeat until you have used all the carrot mixture. Sprinkle with feta and serve with lemon wedges on the side.

POTATO AND SALAMI CHEESECAKE

This makes an original appetizer dish for a fancy dinner, plays an excellent sideman to a light main course, and also makes a great lunch with some roasted squash or a simple salad as a side.

SERVES 8

3 pounds waxy gold potatoes, such as Yukon Gold

4 tablespoons (½ stick) unsalted butter

1 cup fresh bread crumbs, toasted in a sauté pan until light golden brown

4 large eggs

½ cup whole milk

¼ cup fresh ricotta

1 cup freshly grated Parmigiano-Reggiano

½ pound sweet Italian salami, cut into ¼-inch dice

1 bunch fresh flat-leaf parsley, finely chopped (¼ cup)

4 ounces Asiago, grated

Place the potatoes in a saucepan and add water to cover. Bring the water to a boil and cook the potatoes until tender, about 45 minutes.

Meanwhile, butter the bottom and sides of a 12-inch springform pan with 2 tablespoons of the butter and dust the bottom and sides with ¼ cup of the bread crumbs.

In a medium bowl, lightly beat the eggs. Add the milk and ricotta and mix; set aside.

Preheat the oven to 400°F.

Drain and peel the potatoes and pass them through a food mill or ricer into a very large bowl. While the potatoes are still warm, use a large rubber spatula to fold in the Parmigiano, then add the salami and the parsley and stir just enough to evenly mix. Gently stir in the egg mixture; do not overstir, just bring it all together.

Place half of the potato mixture in the prepared pan and gently smooth it to the edges. Sprinkle the grated Asiago over the potato mixture to within ¼ inch of the outer edge, but not over. Top with the remaining potato mixture and carefully smooth it over with a wet spatula. Sprinkle with the remaining ¾ cup bread crumbs and dot with the remaining 2 tablespoons butter. Place the pan on a baking sheet and bake for 25 to 30 minutes, until light golden brown on top. Remove from the oven and let rest for 20 minutes.

Unmold onto a serving plate and cut into wedges like a cheesecake to serve.

JALAPEÑO-ROBIOLA POPPERS

MAKES 24 POPPERS

Olive oil, for the pan

2 large eggs

¼ cup half-and-half

1 tablespoon kosher salt

1 cup panko bread crumbs

1 tablespoon freshly ground
    black pepper

1 cup all-purpose flour

1 tablespoon celery salt

8 ounces fresh robiola, straight from
    the fridge

1½ cups shredded mozzarella

Leaves from 1 bunch fresh basil, cut
    into chiffonade (about ¼ cup)

1 teaspoon ground cayenne

12 jalapeños, halved lengthwise,
    stemmed, and seeded

Although there is a TV in almost every local bar in Italy, there is no culture of sports bars like we have across the United States. This is my Italian take on my very favorite sports bar snack. You can substitute any soft creamy cheese for the robiola.

Preheat the oven to 350°F. Brush a baking sheet with olive oil and set aside.

In a small bowl, beat together the eggs, half-and-half, and salt. In a shallow dish, combine the panko and the black pepper. In a separate dish, combine the flour and the celery salt.

In a bowl, stir together the robiola, mozzarella, basil, and cayenne. Spread 1 tablespoon of the cheese mixture into the cavity of each jalapeño half. One at a time, dredge the stuffed jalapeños in the flour mixture, dip them into the egg mixture, then finally dredge them in the seasoned panko, pressing to coat. Place the coated peppers, cut side up, on the prepared baking sheet and bake for about 30 minutes, or until deep golden brown on top. Transfer to a serving platter and serve warm.

New York

Chef:
DAN DROHAN, OTTO ENOTECA
AND PIZZERIA

Farmer:
TIM STARK, ECKERTON HILL FARM

Ingredient:
TOMATOES

Tim Stark is worried about his kohlrabi seedlings. They were planted too close together, and he isn't sure they'll ever reach maturity. He can't do anything about it. He's fretting.

As we walk around Eckerton Hill Farm, set on a hillside two hours west of New York City, he shows us the Revolutionary War–era farmhouse. He points out assorted greens, an herb garden, and an impressive collection of chile peppers. He's excited about a chile with the fruity flavor of a habanero without the devastating heat. And that kohlrabi.

Tim Stark is burying the lead.

The house is beautiful, the peppers delicious, the herbs gorgeous. The kohlrabi will be fine. Even if it isn't, its absence won't cause tremors in the New York markets.

New York's markets do, however, have a keen interest in Tim's tomato plants.

All 38,000 of them.

During the height of the season, he sends up to seven tons of heirloom tomatoes to New York every week. His are the tomatoes of choice at the city's top restaurants and customer favorites at farmers' markets.

Chef Dan Drohan has a standing order for Otto Enoteca and Pizzeria, where the tomatoes are the definitive ingredient in the Caprese salad. Every Italian restaurant has a Caprese, right?

Not like this one. Tim's tomatoes provide an artist's palette. Dan starts with slices of large yellow and variegated green tomatoes. He adds quarters of oblong bright yellow, red, and green varieties. He sprinkles basil and chunks of mozzarella di bufala before garnishing with halved cherry-size tomatoes in any aforementioned tone, plus orange and deep, dark purple. It's part Caprese, part kaleidoscope.

Dan collects the tomato scraps, squeezes them, and adds the juice to the salad's vinaigrette. Too much work went into those tomatoes to waste anything.

It's late September. The tomato plants at Eckerton Hill have been going strong for months.

So has Tim.

They're starting to look a little spent.

So is Tim.

But the plants will keep producing right up until the first frost of the season.

So will Tim.

Tim was working as a consultant in New York when he started 3,000 tomato plants in his Brooklyn apartment one spring. Given the dearth of farmland in Brooklyn, he moved those plants to his family's land in Lenhartsville, Pennsylvania. Tim documented his transition to farming in a 2008 book, *Heirloom*. Spoiler alert: The book ends with allusions to Tim's doubts about owning farmland.

On cue, the next two seasons were banner years, and Tim found himself at an auction bidding on more land.

A lot of the farmland in the area is covered with soybeans and corn, crops that those farmers say feed the world. Respectfully but pointedly, they questioned Tim on the value of a few acres of vegetables.

It's true, Tim admits. Those crops go around the globe and come back as high-fructose corn syrup, soybean oil, and biodiesel. That's fine. Tim just thinks there's value in feeding the eighty Oley Valley families in Eckerton Hill's CSA program every week, too.

Plus, all those Capreses at Otto.

Tim says he grows the second-best tomato you can get. He says the best would come from your backyard. Some of his customers disagree.

Buy a pint of cherry tomatoes from Tim and it's a challenge to find two that are the same size, shape, and color. He isn't sure how many unique varieties he grows, but estimates it's between seventy and eighty.

Try finding that many in someone's backyard.

Tim says the secret to superior tomatoes is soil filled with rich, organic material. But anyone who entertains an idyllic vision of organic farming was absent the first day.

The first day is dirty.

A neighbor offered to let Tim grow on his seven-acre plot. The neighbor couldn't farm anymore and wanted an organic crop on the land that would stand out among all that corn, being grown to feed the world.

It's going to take some work.

The land is in decent shape, but needs to be cleaned up. It's weedy, with remnants of the last crops grown here—chard and carrots—shooting up indiscriminately.

Building dirt starts with a mushroom compost. This isn't shiitake stems and portobello scraps. This is what mushrooms *grow* in. "Mushroom compost" sounds nice, but make no mistake: It's a big load of horse and chicken manure.

It makes you wonder if anything is truly vegan.

Tim has a six-foot-high pile of compost covering an area about the size of a basketball court. To spread that over the field will take three people, a front-end loader, two tractors, and two spreaders, specialty trailers with parallel helix blades exposed at the back end. It looks like something you might take a hayride on…if Freddy Krueger were the farmer.

Tim runs the loader, depositing compost in the spreaders. With each scoop, white wisps rise from the pile. The compost has been here for a week. It's barely 50 degrees this morning, yet the process of decomposition leaves the interior of this mound hot to the touch.

It's a steaming pile of, well, *organic matter.*

The tractors cover the field, the spreader blades breaking up compost and flinging it into the air in a cloud of dust. This heavy-metal dance continues until the piles are gone. Everyone is covered in a light dusting of… Maybe it's best not to think about it.

Tomorrow, Tim will plow the compost into the soil. Later, he'll till the field to break everything up and mix it in. After all that, the ground will still not be ready to grow Tim's tomatoes. But it *will* be ready to grow clover and rye. In the spring, he'll plow them into the soil. Clover pumps up the nitrogen—tomatoes love nitrogen—and rye's root system adds more organic matter.

Now the neighbor's land is ready to grow Tim's tomatoes. But only about a third of it. He'll leave cover crops on the rest and rotate his tomatoes each season. The part he'll plant should mean 7,000 more tomato plants next year.

That could be an extra ton of tomatoes for New York every week.

Caprese, anyone?

SPICY RICOTTA AND TOMATO

"In Carozza"

This is my mash-up of a grilled cheese sammie and the simple tomato sandwich of my childhood. The true keys are the perfection of the tomatoes and the excessive use of black pepper.

MAKES 4 SERVINGS

1 pound fresh ricotta

8 (½-inch-thick) slices firm whole wheat bread

Maldon sea salt or some other crunchy, shale-y salt

Freshly cracked black pepper—lots

2 ripe large heirloom tomatoes

2 large eggs

½ cup whole milk

1 tablespoon sugar

1 teaspoon ground cayenne

1 teaspoon kosher salt

Grating of nutmeg

4 tablespoons extra-virgin olive oil

2 tablespoons unsalted butter

Evenly spread the ricotta on 4 slices of the bread. Sprinkle with Maldon salt and crack a lot of fresh pepper over the ricotta. Cut the tomatoes into 1-inch-thick slices, then cut the slices into half-moons. Lay the tomatoes on top of the ricotta, covering the ricotta nearly to the edges, then sprinkle the tomatoes with more Maldon salt. Cover with the 4 remaining slices of bread to form sandwiches. Trim the crusts off and cut each sandwich into 4 equal finger-shaped pieces.

In a wide, shallow bowl, whisk the eggs. Add the milk, sugar, cayenne, kosher salt, and nutmeg and whisk until well blended.

In a 10- to 12-inch nonstick sauté pan, heat 2 tablespoons of the olive oil over medium-high heat until smoking. Add 1 tablespoon of the butter and cook until the sizzling subsides. Dip 8 of the sandwich pieces into the egg mixture, turning to coat well, then place them in the pan and cook until golden brown on the first side, about 2 minutes. Flip the sandwiches over and cook until golden brown on the other side, about 2 minutes more. Transfer the sandwiches to a plate, and repeat the process with the remaining 2 tablespoons olive oil, 1 tablespoon butter, and 8 sandwich fingers. Arrange provocatively and serve.

SWEET CORN– PARMIGIANO BUDINO

This is simply the finest, creamiest, richest, and most decadent appetizer pudding you will ever taste. Prepare yourself to experience joy.

MAKES 8 (6-OUNCE) PORTIONS

2 tablespoons unsalted butter

4 ears corn

1 tablespoon kosher salt

½ teaspoon freshly grated nutmeg

2 tablespoons extra-virgin olive oil

1½ cups freshly grated
  Parmigiano-Reggiano

2 cups heavy cream

4 extra-large eggs

1 teaspoon cornstarch

1 teaspoon freshly cracked black
  pepper

Preheat the oven to 325°F. Grease eight 6-ounce ramekins with the butter and set aside.

Place a kettle of water on the stove to boil.

Remove the kernels from the corncobs, place them in a bowl, and season with the salt and nutmeg.

In a cast-iron skillet, heat the olive oil over medium-high heat until smoking.

Dump the corn kernels into the skillet and sauté/char quickly, stirring continuously, for about 2 minutes, then remove and let cool.

In a large bowl, whisk together the Parmigiano, cream, eggs, and cornstarch to form a batter, then stir in the charred corn kernels and the pepper.

Portion the batter evenly among the buttered ramekins and place them in a roasting pan in the oven. Fill the pan with hot water from the kettle to within ½ inch of the top of the ramekins and bake for 20 minutes. Rotate the pan 180 degrees and cook for 20 minutes more. Remove, allow to cool, and serve. (These can be refrigerated for up to 24 hours and served cool or at room temperature.)

SWISS CHARD SPANAKOPITA PIE

I love the classic mini spanakopita with spinach, but I think this version has more confidence and a lot of the slightly bitter flavor I love about cruciferous heroes. The French feta is the best feta for me in this dish, but Greek or even domestic will work nicely.

SERVES 6 TO 8

3 tablespoons olive oil

2 small onions, cut into ⅛-inch dice

4 cloves garlic, smashed

3 pounds Swiss chard, washed and spun dry, leaves cut into 1-inch ribbons, stems chopped

1 teaspoon freshly grated nutmeg

½ cup freshly grated Pecorino Romano

½ cup panko bread crumbs

8 ounces feta, crumbled (I prefer the mild French kind)

½ cup pine nuts

Kosher salt and freshly ground black pepper

6 large eggs

6 sheets from 1 package phyllo dough, defrosted, unrolled, and held on a baking sheet under a damp towel

8 tablespoons (½ cup) unsalted butter, melted

Preheat the oven to 375°F. You will need a 9-by-13-inch baking pan or baking dish.

Heat a spaghetti pot or Dutch oven over medium heat. Add the olive oil, onions, and garlic and sauté until soft and golden brown, about 10 minutes. Add the chard, stir to combine, cover with a lid, and cook until fully cooked and tender, about 15 minutes. Check the pot every 5 minutes and stir to get the raw chard on the top down to the bottom. Drain in a colander and let cool.

Place the cooked chard in a large bowl and add the nutmeg, Pecorino, bread crumbs, feta, and pine nuts and mix well. Add salt and pepper to taste. Crack the eggs into a separate bowl, whisk, then add the eggs to the chard mixture and stir gently until fully combined.

Separate 6 sheets of the phyllo from the pile and place them on your work surface. Fold each sheet in half to create a 9-by-13-inch double-thick sheet (most phyllo is sold in 18-by-13-inch pieces).

Brush some melted butter on the bottom of your 9-by-13-inch pan, spread 1 folded sheet of phyllo onto the buttered bottom, and brush the top of the doubled sheet with melted butter. Repeat this with 2 more doubled sheets (for a total of 3 sheets). Spoon the chard filling over this layer of phyllo, then cover with 3 more doubled sheets, buttering the top of each as you go. Score the top 3 sheets with a sharp knife to create nice diamond shapes. Bake for 45 to 50 minutes, until the top is golden brown, then remove and let rest for 15 minutes.

Cut the spanakopita into 2-inch squares and serve.

ZUCCHINI AND MOZZARELLA FRITTERS

SERVES 4; MAKES 16 TO 18 FRITTERS

2 medium zucchini or yellow squash

2 cloves garlic, thinly sliced

½ cup thinly sliced scallions (4 to 5 scallions)

8 ounces mozzarella, cut into ¼-inch cubes

1 tablespoon freshly ground black pepper

1 teaspoon kosher salt

Zest of 2 lemons

3 large eggs, beaten

¾ cup self-rising flour

¼ cup olive oil

1 lemon, cut into wedges

These crisp little heroes are an excellent way to use up the excessive bounty of the end-of-harvest squash crop. Like an arancino, the mozzarella melts and becomes magnificently stringy as you bite in and pull away the remaining piece… wheeeeeee!

Grate the zucchini on the large holes of a box grater into a bowl. Add the garlic, scallions, and mozzarella and stir to mix well. Add the pepper, salt, lemon zest, and eggs and stir to combine. Add the flour and stir gently until just barely mixed.

In a 12- to 14-inch frying pan, heat the oil until it registers 375°F on a deep-fry thermometer, or just under the smoking point. Scoop 2-tablespoon dollops of the zucchini mixture and gently drop them into the hot oil. Being careful not to crowd the pan, add three to four more dollops. Cook until golden brown, about 2 minutes, flip with a spatula, and cook on the second side until golden brown, about 2 minutes more. Transfer to paper towels to drain and repeat with the remaining zucchini mixture.

Place the fritters on a serving platter with lemon wedges and serve.

Washington, D.C.

Chef:
JOSÉ ANDRÉS, JALEO

Farmer:
JIM CRAWFORD, NEW MORNING FARM

Ingredients:
SWEET CORN, LEEKS, BERRIES

Chef José Andrés scans the tables at the New Morning Farm stand, choosing the best of the week's harvest on the first cool day of fall in Washington, D.C.

He grabs an armload of large leeks and hoists them onto his shoulder as his assistant inspects the cauliflower. Shoppers tell him how much they love his restaurants, his books, his television show. He's quick with tips on how to cook the beans on display, or what sights to see in Spain.

At his restaurants, he serves spherified liquid olives and snowballs that taste like a mojito, but today he makes a passionate case—with José, every case is passionate—for the simplicity of a spinach salad with chickpeas.

He picks up greens, mushrooms, red peppers. He asks his assistant to take a 40-pound box of tomatoes over to the cashier. She says she can't carry it, so he gives her a hand.

She says they should get pumpkins, and flowers, because Mommy would like them.

His assistant is his daughter Lucia. She's nine. José isn't here shopping for his restaurants. This is all going home.

José has known the farmer at this stand for two decades. He credits him for instilling an enthusiasm for local produce.

But at this stand, everyone knows the farmer.

Jim Crawford also has a constant stream of people jockeying for position to talk to him. What's good this week? Is corn season over? Will there still be tomatoes next week?

Jim has been farming in central Pennsylvania since the 1970s. One of the first things he learned was that there are a lot of farmers in the area, but not a lot of customers. He was about two hours north of Washington, where there are a lot of customers, but not many farms. Each week, he drove down and sold whatever he could load onto his truck.

Chefs started buying from him. A lot. It was hard for him to grow enough to supply restaurants, and his neighbors couldn't fill the demand, either.

So they started the Tuscarora Organic Growers Cooperative, which handles logistics for about fifty farmers in the region. Now the farmers concentrate on growing some 1,200 varieties of vegetables, and the co-op delivers to more than sixty Washington-area restaurants.

On Saturdays, Jim still makes the trip to D.C. His farm stand, at a small school in a neighborhood about four miles from the White House, is his stage. He is equal parts host, old pal, farmer, ringleader, choreographer, and pitchman. He knows many customers by name, asks how mothers are doing, and gives personalized updates on favorite crops. But this is just a small part of his job. Here is one farmer's almanac:

WINTER: The year starts slow in the fields at New Morning Farm. There are a few winter farmers' markets, but the inventory is mostly things that were harvested in the fall: cabbage, beets, potatoes.

By February, it's still cold, but it's time to start planting. Spring crops such as peppers, cucumbers, and onions—"garden-variety crops," Jim says, without a note of irony—can be started in the greenhouse, where they will grow until the ground is ready for them. Plants that will fill acres in a few weeks need just a few square feet of greenhouse space right now.

In the fields are plastic-covered structures, where he can start growing lettuce. From now until October, Jim's crew will plant up to 3,000 heads every week.

SPRING: Things get fast and furious. Seedlings from the greenhouse are transplanted into the fields. But that's still a gamble. Frost is still possible, so Jim studies weather patterns and forecasts. Right now, farming is all about calculating risk.

By the end of April, most of the crops that New Morning grows are in production. It's a busy month, but it's the month during which, maybe more than any other, a farmer is a farmer.

Then the dancing starts. A farmer needs to harvest as much as can be sold in a week, then harvest that much again the next week.

Jim calculates how many plants it will take for the yield he needs, how long it will take those plants to mature, how long they will bear, when they'll die, when he needs to plant again for an uninterrupted supply, and how the weather could alter his plan.

Then he has to do it again for each of his sixty-some crops.

By June, the season opens for Jim's farm stand in Washington. A picnic table in the school yard is groaning with strawberries. It seems an endless supply.

"I can't believe the strawberries," a worried-looking member of Jim's crew tells him.

"That's all we have left?" Jim asks.

As many as there are, it's a fraction of what they started the day with. And in just a couple of hours, the seemingly endless supply is gone.

SUMMER: It's 11:30 a.m. on a Saturday, and Jim has been at the market for five hours. The crops are at their peak, and so are the crowds. There are still a few hours before the market closes, and there's no time for lunch.

Jim walks over to the overflowing table of corn, grabs an ear, pulls back the husk, and takes a bite. Then another.

He's eating the profits!

A woman standing nearby sees him and starts loading a bag with corn.

"A dollar off a dozen ears!" Jim calls out. A couple more ears go in the bag.

So maybe he just profited by eating.

Before fall starts, the winter squash are ready. Sort of.

Unlike other crops on the farm, winter squash are planted all at once and harvested all at once. They go into crates where they continue to ripen, getting sweeter in storage. They'll go to market through the holidays.

FALL: Planting is mostly over for the season. There's still plenty to harvest, but any summer crop still in the field will be wiped out when the frosts start.

That's okay. It's normal.

"Normal" is the best weather that a farmer can ask for, Jim says. An extended summer benefits some crops, but at the expense of something that needs cool weather.

So bring it on.

As the market season wanes, big sellers are cauliflower, broccoli, leeks, those winter squash: things that were harvested earlier but will keep awhile.

Planning is underway for next year. It all starts over.

CHERRY MOSTARDA

with Prosciutto

SERVES 8

2 cups dried cherries

½ cup dried cranberries

3 cups moscato d'Asti or other sweet muscat-based wine (even sweet Riesling)

2 cups sugar

¼ cup English mustard powder, such as Colman's

2 tablespoons mustard seeds

1 tablespoon red pepper flakes

2 tablespoons mustard oil (optional)

½ pound prosciutto, thinly sliced at your deli

Mostarda *refers to a hundred different spiced fruit compotes used all over Veneto and Lombardia as a condiment for anything from bollito misto,* to a cheese course, to, in this case, cured meats. It makes an excellent way to jazz up tomorrow's sandwich, but I will often just dip a teaspoon in mid-afternoon for a zippy pick-me-up.

In a medium saucepan, combine the cherries and cranberries and stir. Add the wine and bring to a boil over medium heat. Lower the heat to maintain a simmer and cook until the wine has reduced to 1 cup, about 30 minutes.

Remove from the heat, add the sugar, mustard powder, mustard seeds, and red pepper flakes and stir to dissolve the sugar. Allow to cool, then cover and let steep for 24 hours at room temperature.

Add the mustard oil (if using), stir, and transfer the mostarda to a jar. Refrigerate if not being used immediately.

Lay the prosciutto out on a cutting board or large platter and serve with the mostarda in a fancy little jar or bowl alongside. (Any remaining mostarda can be refrigerated for at least a week.)

FAVA BEAN GUACAMOLE

SERVES 6 TO 8

2 tablespoons kosher salt

2 pounds fava beans, shelled

6 scallions, minced

½ small red onion, cut into ⅛-inch dice

¼ cup chopped fresh cilantro

1 jalapeño, cut into ⅛-inch dice

Zest and juice of 1 lime

2 tablespoons extra-virgin olive oil

Coarse sea salt, such as Maldon

Tortilla chips or crudités, for serving

Unctuous favas mimic avocados here and actually make the guac a little bit more interesting for me. The rest of the ingredients for this classic Mexican dish are the same, so test your friends' palates by asking if they can guess the recipe's secret ingredient!

Bring 6 quarts of water to a boil and add the kosher salt. Set up an ice bath with 4 quarts of cold water and 2 cups of ice.

Boil the favas until tender, about 2 minutes. Drain and shock them in the ice bath. Drain again and gently pinch the ends with a finger and thumb to break the skin and push out the bean. Place the skinned favas and all the remaining ingredients into a molcajete or a mortar and pestle (or just a nice bowl) and mash just until a little chunky. Season with coarse sea salt and serve immediately with tortilla chips and/or crudités.

PROSCIUTTO, GOAT CHEESE,
and Green Bean Roll-Ups

I am always looking for passed appetizers that do not look like I hired a caterer, but that taste and look beautiful on their own merit. Let me introduce to you…

MAKES 16 ROLL-UPS

2 tablespoons plus ¼ cup extra-virgin olive oil

2 pounds fresh thin green beans or haricots verts, trimmed

Kosher salt and freshly ground black pepper

16 slices prosciutto San Daniele or nice, thinly sliced American ham

1 cup fresh soft goat cheese

¼ cup pure, grade A maple syrup

1 teaspoon Chinese-style hot mustard

¼ cup red wine vinegar

1 bunch scallions, thinly sliced

Preheat the oven to 450°F.

Drizzle the 2 tablespoons of oil onto a baking sheet and spread the beans over in a single layer. Season the beans with salt and pepper. Roast until just starting to get a little wrinkled and golden brown, about 10 minutes. Remove and let cool.

Lay the prosciutto slices on a clean work surface and place 1 tablespoon of the goat cheese at the base of each slice. Place 4 or 5 cooked beans over the goat cheese and roll forward to create a bundle and arrange the rolls on a nice platter. In a small bowl, whisk together the maple syrup, mustard, and vinegar until smooth, then drizzle in the remaining ¼ cup olive oil to create a smooth sauce.

When ready to serve, top each bundle with a bit of the sauce and sprinkle with scallions. Serve cool.

Two:
OYSTERS

FRIED OYSTERS

with Rémoulade

My fave version of this dish on the entire planet is served at Pearl Oyster Bar in New York's West Village, where Chef Rebecca Charles makes the best tartar sauce of all. I modified the recipe, but when I eat this, I am back on Cornelia Street, dreaming about New Orleans.

MAKES 2 DOZEN FRIED OYSTERS

FOR THE RÉMOULADE

1½ cups mayonnaise

¼ cup Creole mustard

Zest and juice of 1 lemon

1 tablespoon pimentón (Spanish paprika)

2 teaspoons prepared horseradish

1 teaspoon sweet pickle juice or sugar

1 teaspoon hot sauce (preferably Tabasco)

2 scallions, minced

1 rib celery, cut into fine brunoise

1 tablespoon tiniest capers, or chopped large capers

FOR THE OYSTERS

2 cups olive oil, for frying

2 dozen large oysters, shucked, bottom shells reserved, washed and dried

1 cup whole milk

¼ cup Frank's RedHot sauce

½ cup all-purpose flour

Freshly ground black pepper

Freshly grated nutmeg

4 egg whites

1 cup finely ground fresh bread crumbs

MAKE THE RÉMOULADE

In a bowl, stir together the mayonnaise, mustard, lemon zest, lemon juice, pimentón, horseradish, pickle juice, Tabasco, scallions, celery, and capers and mix well. Cover and refrigerate for at least 1 hour.

MAKE THE OYSTERS

In a heavy saucepan or deep fryer, heat the oil until it registers 365°F on a deep-fry thermometer. While the oil heats, arrange the reserved oyster shells on a nice tray and place a teaspoon of the rémoulade in each. Set aside.

Set up a breading station: In a bowl, mix together the milk and Frank's RedHot. In a separate bowl, season the flour with pepper and nutmeg. In a third bowl, whip the egg whites until slightly foamy. Place the bread crumbs in a shallow dish.

Pick through the oysters to make sure there are no shell pieces attached and place them in the milk mixture. Remove one oyster, shake it dry, and dredge it in the seasoned flour. Remove, shake off any excess, and dredge the oyster in the egg whites. Remove, shake off any excess, and dredge in the bread crumbs. Continue until all the oysters are breaded. Place 6 oysters at a time in the hot oil and fry until they are dark golden brown, 1 to 2 minutes.

Using a slotted spoon, remove the oysters from the hot oil and touch them to a paper towel to drain, then place 1 fried oyster on top of the rémoulade in each oyster shell and serve.

RAW OYSTERS

with Three Sauces: Mignonette, Cocktail, and Horseradish Granita

Raw oysters are a joy, and you can make any one of these sauces for a quick snack—or make all three and have an oyster party. Fill a sink or a bucket with ice, load the oysters in to chill for an hour, and teach everyone how to shuck and jive.

MIGNONETTE SAUCE

2 shallots, minced

¾ cup good champagne vinegar or white wine vinegar

1 tablespoon sugar

1 teaspoon freshly ground black pepper

1 tablespoon chopped fresh dill

Place the shallots, vinegar, and sugar in a small saucepan and bring to a boil. Cook for 1 minute, then remove from the heat and let cool to room temperature. Add the pepper and dill. Serve in a small bowl with an espresso spoon, near the oysters.

MAKES 1 CUP

COCKTAIL SAUCE

1 cup ketchup

3 tablespoons prepared horseradish

Juice of 1 lemon

1 teaspoon Worcestershire sauce

1 teaspoon chipotle hot sauce (I like Tabasco Chipotle Sauce)

In a small bowl, stir together the ketchup, horseradish, lemon juice, Worcestershire, and chipotle sauce. Serve in a small bowl with an espresso spoon, near the oysters.

MAKES 1½ CUPS

Continued on page 49.

HORSERADISH GRANITA SAUCE

1 cup chopped peeled fresh
    horseradish

½ cup rice vinegar

3 cups water

3 tablespoons sugar

Pinch of salt

In a blender, combine the horseradish, vinegar, and 1 cup of the water; blend until pureed. Hold your head away from the blender when you open it—the horseradish has some real kick! Transfer the mixture to a large bowl, stir in the remaining 2 cups water, then let stand for 10 minutes. Strain the mixture through a fine-mesh sieve into a bowl, pressing down firmly to extract the liquid from the solids. Discard the solids. Add the sugar and salt and stir until they dissolve. Pour the granita mixture into a wide, shallow container (the shallower the container, the quicker the granita will freeze), such as a stainless-steel baking pan.

Cover and freeze the mixture for 1 to 2 hours, until it is solid around the edges. Take the container out of the freezer and scrape the ice with a fork, mixing it from the edges into the center.

Repeat this scraping and mixing process every 30 minutes or so (at least three times), until the entire mixture has turned into small flakes. When ready to serve, scrape with a fork to loosen the granita, spoon into a serving dish, and serve next to the oysters.

MAKES 3½ CUPS

OYSTER AND SHRIMP PO'BOY

My favorite po'boy in the Big Easy is at Domilise's Po-Boy & Bar on Annunciation Street. This is my take on their best sammie of all. Sadly, Miss Dot passed away recently, may she rest her soul in culinary heaven.

SERVES 4

4 cups peanut oil, for frying

1 cup all-purpose flour

3 tablespoons Old Bay seasoning

2 large eggs

½ cup Texas Pete hot sauce

16 medium shrimp, peeled and deveined

16 oysters, shucked

4 soft hoagie rolls

1 cup Rémoulade (page 44)

2 ripe tomatoes, thinly sliced

¼ head iceberg lettuce, shredded

Kosher salt and freshly ground black pepper

Splash of red wine vinegar

Heat the oil in a high-sided pot until it registers 365°F on a deep-fry thermometer.

Place the flour and Old Bay in a shallow bowl and mix well. In a small bowl, beat the eggs, then add the hot sauce and beat again.

Dip the shrimp into the egg mixture, letting any excess drip off, then dredge them in the flour mixture.

Place the shrimp in the oil, one at a time, and cook until golden brown, about 1 minute. Using a slotted spoon, remove the shrimp and drain on paper towels. Repeat with the remaining shrimp.

Dredge the oysters in the flour mixture and carefully drop them into the oil one at a time. Fry until golden, about 1 minute. Drain on paper towels.

Assemble the sandwiches: Split and toast the rolls, then spread both sides of the bread with some of the rémoulade. Divide the sliced tomatoes among the rolls, then the shredded lettuce. Season with salt and pepper and a splash of vinegar. Place 4 oysters and 4 shrimp on top of the lettuce in each sandwich and close. Serve immediately.

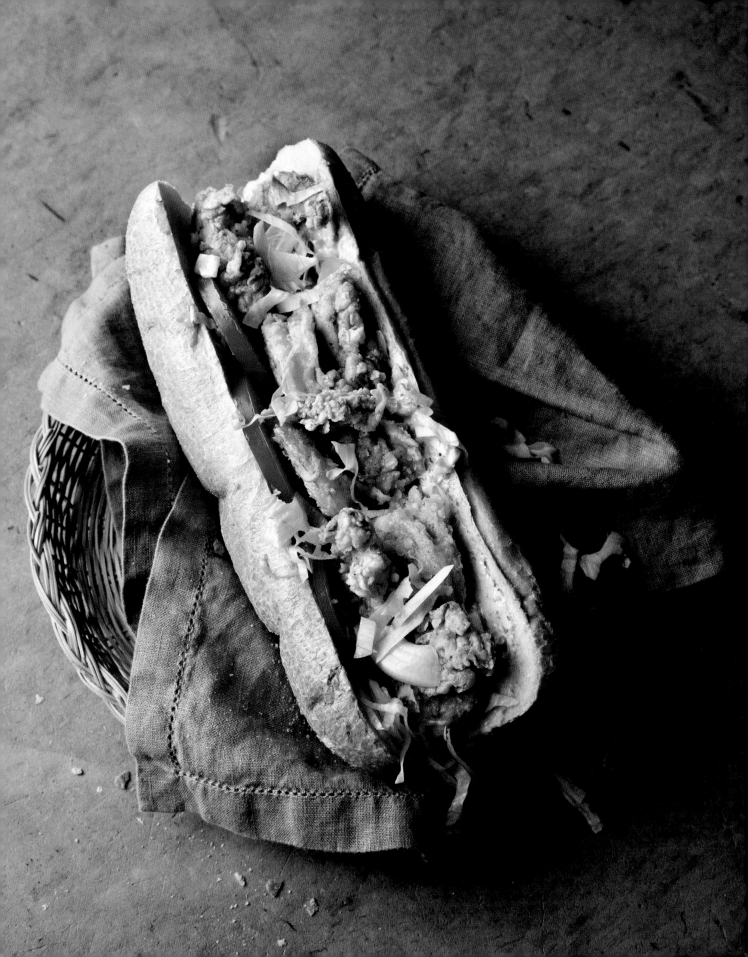

BBQ OYSTERS

As a boy in Seattle, my family and I used to head out to Hood Canal and pick as many wild Washington oysters as we could find. Barbecuing the oysters was the simplest and best way to eat a lot of them, and man, oh man, we would.

SERVES 4 TO 6

Rock salt, for serving

8 tablespoons (1 stick) unsalted butter, at room temperature

4 cloves garlic, mashed

1 bunch fresh flat-leaf parsley, finely chopped (¼ cup)

2 tablespoons Cocktail Sauce (page 46), at room temperature

2 tablespoons Crystal hot sauce

24 oysters, scrubbed

Preheat the grill or barbecue. Spread rock salt evenly on a serving tray.

Place the butter and garlic in a small saucepan and melt the butter over low heat. Add the parsley, cocktail sauce, and hot sauce, transfer to a small bowl, and set aside.

Shuck the oysters and carefully loosen them from the bottom shell, leaving the oyster on the half-shell. Place a scant teaspoon of the butter mixture on top of each oyster and then place them on the grill, shell side down, and cook until the oysters bubble and curl up at the edges.

Place the cooked oysters, still in their shells, on the rock salt–lined tray, and serve.

Rockland

Chef:
MELISSA KELLY, PRIMO

Farmer:
JEFF "SMOKEY" MCKEEN,
PEMAQUID OYSTER COMPANY

Ingredient:
OYSTERS

When Melissa Kelly's staff at Primo in Rockland, Maine, need herbs, they walk out the kitchen door and pick them.

The microgreens are across the parking lot, next to the 250 laying hens that supply the restaurant's eggs.

Up a hill—past roaming guinea hens and ducks and the pen for the pigs—there's a garden where they grow most of their vegetables.

In the kitchen, her team cranks out pasta for the night's menu next to the room where she cures salumi.

Primo is a model of self-sufficiency.

Even so, there are things she farms out. She buys onions and potatoes from local farmers because she uses so many.

And she doesn't raise her own oysters.

There are a lot of oystermen in Maine, and Melissa buys from several. But she was serving oysters from Jeff "Smokey" McKeen and Pemaquid Oyster Company when she worked in New York. So when she moved to Maine, Smokey became one of her go-to vendors.

On a day off, she went down to Pemaquid to see the operation. She asked her staff if anyone wanted to join her.

All of them did.

In shifts, they went out on Smokey's small boat to see what goes into raising oysters.

Luckily, Smokey likes to give the tour.

It's a sunny Sunday in September, and Smokey is helping shuck 20,000 oysters for the festival he's cohosting on the Damariscotta River. His name tag says "Oyster Czar," a title he earned after he banned cocktail sauce from the festival. He stands out in the festival crowd, if not for his audacious title, then for his shock of toasted hair and thick goatee.

Someone asks for a tour, so he drops his knife and walks the group along a floating dock. It feels like walking in a video game. The dock shifts and sways and dips; there are no rails, and it seems possible that the dock might disappear from under your feet at any moment. Game over.

He says this year's crop of 1.5 million oysters arrived a few months ago in a bucket a little bigger than a paint can. He points to places on the dock and talks about sorting and grading and feeding and circulating. It all seems hypothetical, like he's pointing out where things happen at some point in time that isn't right now, since all we see are shaky docks. He

suddenly lifts a trapdoor in the dock, drops down prone, and reaches an arm into the 68-degree water. He grabs a handful of what look like unkempt fingernail trimmings and explains that they've grown by fifty percent in a couple of weeks.

In his palm, he's holding two dozen oysters, each smaller than a dime. This time next year, someone will pay $40 for these at the festival. Smokey's quick demonstration makes clear something he assumed we already realized: Attached to the underside of those shaky docks are dozens of crates. Each contains thousands of fledgling oysters.

It's all happening beneath our feet. We're standing on an oyster farm.

Back at the festival, poets have finished reciting oyster-themed contest entries, and the folk band Old Grey Goose takes the stage. Smokey is the band's guitarist/accordionist/vocalist/folklorist/researcher.

The band's first song is about mussels, and singer Carter Newell, one of Smokey's partners in Pemaquid, apologizes, assuring the crowd that the rest of the songs will be about oysters.

Despite the oyster's reputation in

amorous matters, things seem rough for the main characters in the songs. In "The Ballad of the Oysterman," lyrics from a poem by Oliver Wendell Holmes Sr., an oysterman notices a girl across the river. She invites him over. Her father, a fisherman, comes home. It doesn't end well for the oysterman.

In another, "Basket of Oysters," author unknown, the main character is an oyster lover trying to buy a basketful from a woman on the street. There's much negotiating. We surmise that the oysters are a metaphor. It still doesn't end well for the oyster lover.

Old Grey Goose has given Smokey and his bandmates the chance to tour the world. As part of a government cultural exchange, they've played in Poland, Uzbekistan, Turkmenistan, Kyrgyzstan, West Africa, Israel, and Jordan. A Catholic group sponsored a trip to Cuba.

Music gave Smokey something else, too: his nickname. Many assume it came from his coif, but he and a friend had a gig at a place where playing under assumed names seemed prudent. He didn't have one, so his cohort, Blind Skeeter, called him Smokey.

From New Brunswick to Damariscotta, Massachusetts, the Chesapeake Bay, over to Apalachicola and on to Louisiana and Texas, locals say their local oysters are best.

Actually, they're all the same oyster: *Crassostrea virginica.*

That doesn't mean they aren't different, though.

Smokey explains that a big part of an oyster's flavor is the liquid in the shell of a well-shucked oyster. That liquor is unique to an area, developed by water temperature, water flow, and what the oyster eats. It tastes a lot like the water from which the oyster was harvested because it mostly *is* the water from which the oyster was harvested.

After a few months at the marina, Smokey takes his oysters about a mile down the Damariscotta, closer to the Atlantic. When they're about the size of a quarter, they are spread out over the riverbed, where they'll grow for a year or more. When they're scooped up—probably half will be recovered— they're ready to eat. Almost.

Smokey takes those oysters farther down the river, just short of the ocean, and suspends them in cold, briny water. The oysters purge the sediment they've fed on and take in clean seawater.

Then they're ready.

Just not for cocktail sauce.

Smokey's fine with a little lemon or hot sauce—even horseradish, in moderation. Mignonettes are welcome. He'll even acquiesce to the cocktail sauce his wife makes.

But when Smokey sees a jar of commercial cocktail sauce at the festival, all brash and overwhelming, he assumes someone planted it to rile him. He considers dumping it into the river below. But he doesn't.

He has more than a million oysters down there.

  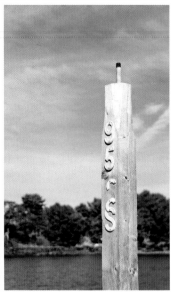

OYSTER PAN ROAST

This rich, decadent, easy soup is fast and transcendent, much like the original version served at the Grand Central Oyster Bar in Grand Central Terminal, the New York City commuter hub. Let there be joy!

SERVES 4 TO 6

20 medium oysters, scrubbed

2 tablespoons unsalted butter

2 cloves garlic, sliced paper thin

1 shallot, finely minced

2 ribs celery, thinly sliced

1½ cups heavy cream

1 cup whole milk

1 teaspoon Worcestershire sauce

2 jiggers sherry

Kosher salt and freshly ground
    black pepper

1 bunch fresh chives, finely sliced

Shuck the oysters over a strainer set over a small bowl to collect their liquor. Set aside the oysters and their liquor.

In a medium saucepan, melt the butter over medium heat. Add the garlic, shallot, and celery and sauté until the vegetables are translucent. Add the cream, milk, and Worcestershire and bring to a boil, then reduce the heat to maintain a high simmer and cook for 5 minutes, or until the mixture coats the back of a spoon. Add the reserved oyster liquor, the oysters, and the sherry and cook for 2 minutes.

Divide among four bowls, season with salt and pepper, sprinkle with chives, and serve.

MEXICAN OYSTER COCKTAIL

Pacific coast Mexico is where my first hangovers were born. This Mexican cocktail helps alleviate them instantly.

SERVES 4 TO 6

4 ripe plum tomatoes

4 scallions, thinly sliced

1 bunch fresh cilantro, chopped

2 tablespoons extra-virgin olive oil

1 teaspoon ground cumin

2 ribs celery, sliced paper thin

2 shallots, finely minced

Zest and juice of 3 limes

2 serrano chiles, finely chopped

24 fresh oysters, scrubbed

Kosher salt

Halve the tomatoes and squeeze the seeds into a bowl (reserve them for Tomato Seed Vinaigrette, page 101), then chop the tomatoes into ¼-inch dice and toss them into a bowl. Add the scallions, cilantro, olive oil, cumin, celery, shallots, lime zest, lime juice, and chiles and mix well, then cover and refrigerate for 1 hour.

Shuck the oysters over a strainer set over a small bowl to collect their liquor. Toss the oysters with their liquor into the mixture and stir gently. Check for seasoning—it may or may not need salt. Serve in clear glasses or seafood cocktail servers.

BLACK RISOTTO

with Oysters and Fennel

SERVES 4

12 fresh oysters, scrubbed

¼ cup extra-virgin olive oil

1 medium Spanish onion, cut into ¼-inch dice

1 bulb fennel, cut into ½-inch dice

1½ cups arborio rice

1 cup dry white wine

4 to 6 cups Vegetable Broth (recipe below)

Kosher salt and freshly ground black pepper

2 tablespoons squid ink

2 tablespoons unsalted butter

¼ cup fennel fronds, chopped

Risotto is intimidating only if you get obsessed with the constant stirring. If you start well with a good soffrito, you really can check in with risotto just every 3 or 4 minutes. The trick in this case is to add the oysters literally in the last 20 seconds, after you take the pan off the heat. You can buy squid ink at your fishmonger or online.

Shuck the oysters over a strainer set over a small bowl to collect their liquor. Set aside the oysters and their liquor.

In a 12- to 14-inch frying pan with 3-inch sides, heat the olive oil over medium heat. Add the onion and fennel and cook until softened but not brown, 6 to 7 minutes. Add the rice and cook, stirring continuously, until opaque, about 2 minutes.

Add the wine and cook for 1 minute, then add the vegetable broth, ladle by ladle, until the rice is covered. Raise the heat to medium-high and continue to cook, stirring intermittently, maintaining the level of the liquid to just about the level of the rice, for 15 minutes. Taste for salt and pepper and season accordingly. Continue cooking until the rice is tender but still al dente. Remove from the heat, add the squid ink and the butter. Stir for 30 seconds to incorporate.

Gently stir in the oysters with their liquor and the fennel fronds and let rest for 1 minute, then serve. Risotto should be wet and settle flat on the plate, with a little liquid edging out from the side.

VEGETABLE BROTH

2 red onions, halved

2 carrots, scrubbed, cut into thirds

4 heads garlic, halved

2 leeks, split and rinsed well

1 bay leaf

4 quarts water

Place the onions, carrots, garlic, leeks, and bay leaf in a stockpot with the water and bring to a boil. Reduce the heat to maintain a simmer and cook until reduced by half, 15 to 20 minutes. Strain out the vegetables in a conical sieve over a large bowl and press firmly to extract all of the juices. Return the liquid to the same pot, set on the stovetop, and return the broth to a simmer to use in the risotto. If not using immediately, let cool and then store in an airtight container in the refrigerator for up to 2 days, or freeze for up to 1 month.

MAKES 2 QUARTS

OYSTER FRITTERS

with Ginger-Soy Dipping Sauce

MAKES 24 FRITTERS

1 cup cake flour

Kosher salt

1 large egg

½ cup plain seltzer, chilled

1 tablespoon extra-virgin olive oil

1 teaspoon ground cayenne

Zest of 1 lemon

6 scallions, finely minced

Peanut oil, for frying

¼ cup sweet soy sauce

¼ cup rice vinegar

2 tablespoons finely grated peeled fresh ginger

2 medium cloves garlic, minced

1 teaspoon sesame oil

24 oysters, shucked, shells cleaned and reserved

Lemon wedges, for serving

Tabasco sauce, for serving

This is a variation of tempura, and the success of the dish is all about the heat of the oil and careful oil/oyster crowd management. Be sure to fry the oysters in uncrowded oil, which is dependent on the surface area of your fry pot, so wider is better in this case.

In a medium bowl, mix together the flour and a pinch of salt and set aside.

Crack the egg into another medium bowl and lightly whisk it, then add the seltzer, olive oil, cayenne, lemon zest, and scallions and whisk until combined.

Add the seltzer mixture to the flour and whisk until smooth. Set aside in a cool place to rest for 1 hour.

Pour peanut oil into a heavy-bottomed pot with 6-inch sides to a depth of 3 inches, and heat over medium-high heat until the oil registers 370°F on a deep-fry thermometer.

In a small mixing bowl, stir together the soy sauce, vinegar, ginger, garlic, and sesame oil.

Working in batches of 8 oysters at a time, fry the oysters: Dip one oyster at a time into the batter, letting any excess drip off, then carefully drop the oyster into the hot oil. Fry the oysters, gently stirring occasionally and turning them with a spider, until the batter is crisp and golden, about 90 seconds, then remove with the spider and transfer to paper towels to drain. Repeat with the remaining oysters, making sure that the oil comes back up to 370°F each time before adding the oysters. Season with salt while still hot.

Serve the oysters in clean, dry oyster shells with a squeeze of fresh lemon, a splash of Tabasco, and the dipping sauce on the side.

Three:
SOUPS AND SALADS

COOL BORSCHT WITH CARAWAY

SERVES 8 TO 10

1 pound medium beets, trimmed and peeled

2 medium onions

2 large carrots

3 tablespoons extra-virgin olive oil

1 tablespoon caraway seeds

Kosher salt and coarsely ground black pepper

½ head green cabbage, shredded

6 cups Vegetable Broth (page 62)

Zest and juice of 1 lemon

2 cups sour cream

2 bunches fresh chives, chopped

It is hard to believe that a vegetable I so loathed as a child is now among my favorites of all. Maybe it was because we used canned beets, or maybe it was just the crazy color and its association with canned cranberry sauce that frightened me, but I never loved a beet until I tried a fresh golden one in San Francisco, and now I am a convert. You can sub golden beets in this recipe for a change of hue.

Working with one vegetable at a time, shred the beets, onions, and carrots on the large holes of a box grater or in a food processor using the grating blade. Set aside 1 cup of the shredded beets.

Place a 6-quart saucepan over medium heat. Add the oil and caraway seeds and heat until the oil is smoking. Add the beets, onions, and carrots, season with salt and pepper, and sauté until the vegetables are soft and muted in color, about 10 minutes. Add the cabbage and cook until wilted, 5 minutes, then add the broth and bring to a boil. Cook for 25 minutes, until all is soft, and check for seasoning. Add the lemon zest and lemon juice. Carefully transfer the mixture to a blender or a food processor and puree until smooth.

Transfer the borscht to a large container, cover, and chill for 2 hours.

To serve, stir in the reserved 1 cup shredded beets and check the seasoning again—cold soup frequently needs more salt. Ladle the borscht into shallow, wide bowls. Crack fresh black pepper over the top, add a dollop of sour cream, and sprinkle with chopped chives.

AJO BLANCO

I first tasted this delicious cousin of gazpacho back in high school and then forgot about it for a couple of decades. Traveling through Spain to make a PBS show with my pal Paltrow, we tasted it at a lunch fiesta—we get goose bumps remembering it. It is simply remarkable and easier than pie.

SERVES 4

1 cup blanched whole almonds

6 (1-inch) slices day-old baguette (you can use fresh—the Spaniards would not)

4 cups water

3 cloves garlic, minced

¼ cup sherry vinegar

4 ice cubes

1 cup extra-virgin olive oil, plus more for serving

Sea salt

12 seedless red grapes, halved

Seeds from 1 pomegranate

Zest of 2 oranges

Put the almonds in a small saucepan, cover with cold water, and bring to a boil. Turn off the heat and let cool for 20 minutes.

Meanwhile, soak the bread in the water.

Drain the almonds, transfer to a blender, and add the garlic, vinegar, and ice cubes. Blend until smooth, about 1 minute.

Remove the bread from the water and squeeze the liquid back into the bowl. Working in batches, slowly add half the bread and its water to the almond mixture and blend until smooth. Pour the mixture into a bowl.

Put the remaining bread and water in the blender, and with the motor running, add the olive oil in a slow stream. Thoroughly combine this emulsion with the almond mixture in the bowl. Season with salt, cover, and refrigerate until cold.

In a bowl, toss the grapes, pomegranate seeds, and orange zest to gently mix, then divide the mixture among four soup bowls. Pour the chilled soup over the fruit and serve, drizzled with a little more olive oil.

SWEET PEPPER AND WHITE BEAN SOUP

The creamy bass notes of white beans play perfectly against the high-hat brightness of the peppers' sweet acidity, extending the spectrum of flavor to the perimeter of yum.

SERVES 6 TO 8

4 cups chicken stock (homemade or low-sodium store-bought)

¼ cup extra-virgin olive oil, plus more for serving

1 large Spanish onion, cut into ¼-inch dice

4 fresh sage leaves

¼ pound pancetta, cut into ¼-inch dice

2 tablespoons tomato paste

3 red bell peppers, seeded and cut into ½-inch dice

2 (15-ounce) cans cannellini or white beans, drained and rinsed

Kosher salt and freshly ground black pepper

In a medium pot, bring the chicken stock to a boil.

In a Dutch oven, heat the extra-virgin olive oil over medium heat until almost smoking. Add the onion, sage, and pancetta. Cook, stirring frequently, for 5 minutes, or until the onion is slightly browned. Mix in the tomato paste and the bell peppers and continue to cook, stirring, for 2 minutes more.

Add the boiling chicken stock to the Dutch oven and return to a boil. Reduce the heat to maintain a simmer and cook for 5 minutes. In small batches, transfer the mixture to a blender or food processor and puree until smooth, then pour into the pot in which you heated the chicken stock. Add the white beans and bring to a boil, then reduce the heat to maintain a simmer and cook for 5 minutes. Season with salt and pepper.

Ladle the soup into bowls and serve with a drizzle of extra-virgin olive oil and freshly cracked pepper.

GAZPACHO

Every year or two, I pronounce that this cold soup should be the next big thing. It is completely healthy, easy to make, vegan, and it stores well for a few days…Maybe a gazpacho council should be developed to extol its virtues. In any case, it is so delicious and so good for you, and takes less than 5 minutes to make.

SERVES 4

2 English cucumbers

1 red bell pepper, seeded and roughly chopped

1 yellow bell pepper, seeded and roughly chopped

2 cloves garlic

2 large, very ripe heirloom tomatoes, quartered

1 tablespoon kosher salt, plus more as needed

1 cup ice cubes

¼ cup sherry vinegar

½ cup water

¾ cup extra-virgin olive oil, plus more as needed

Freshly ground black pepper

3 slices American white bread, cut into ¼-inch cubes

1 pint mixed Sun Gold and red cherry tomatoes, halved

1 bunch fresh chives, cut into 1-inch batons (optional)

Pinch of red pepper flakes (optional)

Cut an unpeeled 3-inch section of cucumber into ¼-inch dice and set aside in a small bowl. Peel and seed the remaining cucumbers, cut into chunks, and place in a big bowl along with the bell peppers, garlic, and tomatoes. Working in batches if necessary, place the vegetables in a food processor along with the salt, ice, vinegar, and water and pulse until liquefied and smooth. When all the vegetables have been pureed, whisk in ½ cup of the oil until shiny, smooth, and glossy. Pour into a large bowl, cover, and refrigerate until very cold. Season with salt and black pepper.

In a nonstick 12-inch sauté pan, heat the remaining ¼ cup oil over medium heat. Add the bread cubes and cook until uniformly golden brown. Transfer to a bowl and keep in a warm place. Place the cherry tomatoes in a bowl and set aside.

Divide the gazpacho evenly among four bowls. Drizzle with a bit of oil and sprinkle with chives and red pepper flakes. Serve the croutons, cucumbers, and cherry tomatoes on the side for each guest to serve themselves.

Austin

Chef:
BRYCE GILMORE, BARLEY SWINE

Farmer:
NATHAN HEATH, PHOENIX FARMS

Ingredients:
BEETS, CARROTS

Years ago, a plane flew over a field at a farm in northern Texas where Nathan Heath was working, strafing it with … something.

Nathan had been born on a farm and had worked on one for most of his life. His family's farm was organic before anyone knew to call it that.

But there had never been planes flying over his family's farm. This was weird.

They're defoliating the field, a coworker told him. It's Agent Orange. It's a weapon of war.

That was how Nathan learned what "conventional" farming was. People ate food from this field. But the air was hard to breathe. It was tangibly toxic.

He lost interest in farming and went to work at a used bookstore.

There, he came across *Deep Economy*, Bill McKibben's 2007 book about deglobalization. The book suggests communities should grow their food. It raises concern about the high average age of farmers. Nathan knew how to farm, he was young, and he wasn't doing it.

Nathan felt guilty.

He wanted to get back into farming, but he was going to do it the way his family had done it. He would buy a few acres and start a farm that could be tended by his immediate family.

He wanted to be able to grow all year. He wanted to grow for a community that appreciated his standards. And he wanted to grow some unusual things, because he didn't want to get bored.

So he looked for farmland near Austin, where the city motto is "Keep it weird," and bought eleven acres in nearby Bastrop.

Nathan brings five boxes of vegetables to Barley Swine, Chef Bryce Gilmore's restaurant in Austin. It's hard to find a place to set down the boxes. The crew is prepping for dinner service and every surface is occupied by people making soup dumplings, shaving mushrooms, or drying cornmeal crackers.

A barstool makes a good landing spot. On top of one of the boxes is a bag of beets. Bryce pulls a couple out. They're a little bit bigger than golf balls.

You've seen bigger beets. Most are, really. It doesn't take much effort to let a beet grow bigger. That means more product to sell.

But to Nathan, it's not worth as much. He wants a beet to taste like a beet, the best beet ever. He says smaller beets are sweeter. They're juicier. Smoother. They're also more expensive. Customers wonder if they're worth the price.

Nathan has a confident response: Try them and see.

Doing things differently is part of Nathan's business model. He could plant on more of his land, but increasing production might make it hard to maintain quality. He could probably manage it if he hired help, or used machinery, but he thinks farmers value their product more when their hands are on it.

Chefs love his carrots. He thinks that in Texas's climate, they taste best in the winter and spring. Some farmers grow them until June. Nathan could, too, but he says they'd taste like carrots from a grocery store. What's the point of that?

He says the secret to his carrots and beets is his soil. He has a laundry list of organic materials—lava sand, fish emulsion, and kelp among them—that he tills into the field each time he's ready to plant. And he has a team of worms making more dirt.

He spends a lot of time with seed catalogs—"farmer porn," he calls them. Next to his primary field, he has a secondary plot where he experiments—he can't help himself. A current obsession is exotic squash. He has a half-dozen kinds growing, and he knows if he can grow it, he can find a chef who will love it.

He's obstinate. He heard peanuts don't grow here, but he thought he could do it. Nathan now confirms: Peanuts don't grow here.

Farmers in Central Texas face a unique set of challenges.

For instance, while it's unusual for a thermometer to hit 135 degrees and just melt, it has happened at Phoenix Farms.

This season, Nathan is having trouble with leaf-footed bugs. The bugs prey on young plants, biting the flower and causing the vegetable to develop improperly. They started on Nathan's tomatoes. Then moved to his cucumbers. Then his squash. Then his peppers.

Leaf-footed bugs are easy to eradicate. With pesticides.

Visions of that airplane all over again.

He looks for other ways to boot the bugs. Turns out, leaf-footed bugs love sunflowers. He plans to grow those off to the side of his crops as bait and knock them out there.

He also strategically avoids pests he doesn't want to have to deal with: He doesn't grow corn because it attracts deer. He doesn't grow melons because he learned raccoons are better than him at telling when they're ripe.

Other problems aren't due to four-footed pests. Vendors bring conventional produce to organic farmers' markets, which devalues his crop. Restaurants that aren't serving his produce name him on their menus to increase their credibility at a cost to his: a diner tastes a vegetable that isn't extraordinary, thinks it's from Phoenix Farms, and wonders what the big deal is.

It's all enough to make a farmer want to curl up with a good seed catalog.

* * *

The sense of responsibility that brought Nathan back to farming now has him recruiting new farmers. So many people have asked him to train them to become farmers that he's building a teaching center on the farm. He has taken classes and found them vague. He wants people to know what they're getting into. He wants to inspire them to do it anyway.

He realizes he's ultimately training his competition, and he's okay with that. "If you know something, you have to share it," he says. "It's better for everyone to have ten farmers farming ten acres each than to have one farmer farming a hundred."

He wants to give his students guidance, but his big plan involves buying more land to sublet to new farmers. Give them infrastructure, reduce startup expenses. Let them see if it's for them.

You won't find them in any seed catalog, but Nathan wants to grow a new crop of farmers.

CHILLED SWEET CORN SOUP

with Horseradish Crème Fraîche

SERVES 4 TO 6

10 ears sweet corn, husked

2 carrots

4 leeks, split and rinsed well, white and light green parts cut into ¼-inch half-moons, dark green parts cut into 1-inch pieces

1 Spanish onion, halved

4 quarts cold water

3 tablespoons extra-virgin olive oil

1 large red onion, cut into ¼-inch dice

1 large Yukon gold potato (about 1 pound), peeled and cut into ½-inch dice

Kosher salt and freshly ground white pepper

1 cup crème fraîche or Greek yogurt

4 tablespoons freshly grated horseradish, plus a piece to grate over the soup

Cool corn soup is practically a luxury item at our house, and this soup is so easy to make that we bask in its luxury 24/7 when it's sweet corn season. I may sneak a mug of this for breakfast with a squeeze of lime or take it in a sippy cup to the beach as a quick lunch on the go.

Using a sharp knife, cut the kernels from the corncobs and place the kernels in a bowl. Using the back of the same knife, scrape the cobs to extract the creamy, intense corn liquid and place into the bowl with the corn. Place the cobs in a stockpot with the carrots, the green parts of the leeks, the Spanish onion, and the water. Bring to a boil and cook until the liquid has reduced to 8 cups. Strain into a large bowl, discarding the solids, and set aside.

In a 6-quart saucepan, heat 2 tablespoons of the oil over medium heat. Add the red onions and the white parts of the leeks and cook until translucent, about 6 minutes.

Add the potato and cook for 3 minutes more, then add the warm corn stock and bring to a boil. Cook until the onions and potatoes are very soft, about 10 minutes. Reserve ½ cup of the kernels for garnish; add the rest and cook until soft, about 4 minutes.

Puree with an immersion blender and season with salt and white pepper. Cover and chill for at least 2 hours.

In a small sauté pan, heat the remaining 1 tablespoon of oil, then add the reserved ½ cup of corn kernels and sauté until slightly browned. Remove from heat.

In a bowl, stir together the crème fraîche and grated horseradish and season with salt.

Remove the soup from the fridge and taste for seasoning. It is often underseasoned when served cold, and we hate that.

Ladle 6 ounces of the cold soup into each soup plate. Place a dollop of the crème fraîche mixture on each, grate a little fresh horseradish over the top, sprinkle with the sautéed corn, and serve.

MINESTRONE GENOVESE

On crisp autumn days, our stomachs beg for sustenance in the form of a thick vegetable soup, and what better way to use the last harvests from our gardens or farmers' markets? I suggest that you make a triple batch of the pesto and freeze two…it will add sunshine to winter suppers and make you smile.

SERVES 10

¼ pound dried borlotti or pinto beans

½ pound dried cannellini or other white beans

¼ cup extra-virgin olive oil, plus more as needed

1 large red onion, cut into ¼-inch dice

2 large carrots, halved lengthwise and cut into ½-inch half-moons

2 medium zucchini, cut into ¼-inch rounds

1 (28-ounce) can whole San Marzano tomatoes, cut into ½-inch dice, juices reserved

6 ribs celery, cut into ¼-inch slices

1 bunch broccoli spigarello, cut into ¼-inch ribbons

2 potatoes, peeled and cut into ½-inch dice

2 leeks, split, rinsed well, and cut into ¼-inch half-moons

8 cups cool water

Kosher salt and freshly ground black pepper

½ cup freshly grated Parmigiano-Reggiano

½ cup Pesto Genovese (recipe follows)

Place the beans in separate bowls, add water to cover, and set aside to soak overnight.

Drain the beans, combine them in a pot, and cover with water. Bring the water to a boil, then reduce the heat to maintain a simmer and cook for about 30 minutes, or until still quite al dente. Set aside to cool in the cooking liquid.

In a large soup pot, heat the oil over medium heat until it shimmers. Add the onion, carrots, zucchini, tomatoes, celery, spigarello, potatoes, and leeks and cook slowly, stirring frequently, for 20 minutes. Drain the beans and add them to the pot with the cool water. Bring to a boil, then reduce the heat to maintain a simmer and cook for 1½ hours, or until the beans are tender. Season aggressively with salt and pepper.

Divide the soup among ten shallow soup bowls and top each with a spoonful of grated Parmigiano, a dollop of pesto, and a drizzle of good olive oil.

Continued on page 84.

PESTO GENOVESE

2 cloves garlic

2½ cups lightly packed fresh basil
leaves

3 tablespoons pine nuts

Generous pinch of Maldon or other
flaky sea salt

6 tablespoons extra-virgin olive oil

¼ cup freshly grated
Parmigiano-Reggiano

3 tablespoons freshly grated Pecorino
Romano

Place the garlic in a food processor and pulse to chop it. Add the basil, pine nuts, and salt and pulse until the basil and nuts are coarsely chopped. With the motor running, quickly drizzle in the oil. Transfer to a small bowl or jar and stir in the Parmigiano and Pecorino Romano. (The pesto can be stored in a tightly sealed jar, topped with a thin layer of extra-virgin olive oil, in the refrigerator for several weeks.)

MAKES ABOUT 1 CUP

TOMATO SOUP

with Goat Cheese Dumplings

The dumplings in this case are often referred to as gnudi, effectively ravioli filling cooked like gnocchi. Once you try these little dumplings in a rich tomato soup, you will never need a grilled cheese again.

SERVES 4 TO 6

FOR THE SOUP

2 tablespoons extra-virgin olive oil

2 tablespoons unsalted butter

1 medium red onion, finely chopped

4 large cloves garlic, thinly sliced

¼ cup chopped sun-dried tomatoes

3 tablespoons all-purpose flour

3 cups low-sodium chicken broth

1 (28-ounce) can whole San Marzano plum tomatoes, pureed, juices reserved

1 tablespoon sugar

1 tablespoon fresh thyme leaves

FOR THE DUMPLINGS

1½ cups fresh soft goat cheese

½ cup freshly grated Parmigiano-Reggiano

3 large eggs

½ teaspoon freshly grated nutmeg

1 teaspoon kosher salt

1 teaspoon freshly ground black pepper

5 tablespoons all-purpose flour, plus more for dredging

Kosher salt and freshly ground black pepper

1 bunch fresh basil, leaves cut into chiffonade, for serving

MAKE THE SOUP

In a 6-quart Dutch oven, heat the oil and butter over medium-low heat until the butter melts. Add the onion, garlic, and sun-dried tomatoes and cook, stirring occasionally, until soft but not browned, about 6 minutes. Add the flour, stir to coat the onion and garlic, and cook for 5 minutes more.

Add the broth, plum tomatoes and their juices, sugar, and thyme and bring to a boil over medium-high heat while stirring the mixture. Reduce the heat to low, cover, and simmer for 40 minutes.

MAKE THE DUMPLINGS

While the soup is simmering, bring a large pot of salted water to a boil. Set up an ice bath.

In a large bowl, mix the goat cheese, Parmigiano, and eggs. Stir in the nutmeg, salt, pepper, and flour. Form the mixture into balls the size of a quarter.

Dredge the formed dumplings in flour to coat, tapping off the excess. Slide the dumplings into the boiling water, being careful not to overcrowd the pot; work in batches if necessary. After they float to the top and have cooked for about 4 minutes, remove the dumplings using a slotted spoon and place them in the ice bath to set. When completely chilled, transfer to a baking sheet and refrigerate.

In a Vitamix or other sturdy blender, blend the soup in batches until smooth. Rinse the pot and return the soup to the pot. Season with salt and pepper. Set the pot over medium heat and return the soup to a rapid simmer. Add the chilled gnudi and cook over medium-low heat for 10 minutes, but do not boil.

Serve warm, with basil chiffonade sprinkled over each serving.

CHILLED PEA AND SCALLION SOUP

I love this soup so much that I can eat it for breakfast. It is greener than green eggs and ham and makes me feel more childish and silly than I do when I am merely childish and silly.

SERVES 6 TO 8

2 tablespoons extra-virgin olive oil, plus 2 tablespoons

2 medium shallots, finely chopped

2 bunches scallions, thinly sliced, white and green parts separated

2 cups Vegetable Broth (page 62)

2 cups shelled fresh green peas

Kosher salt and freshly ground black pepper

6 to 8 pieces nice country bread

12 fresh mint leaves, cut into chiffonade

In a heavy-bottomed saucepan, heat 2 tablespoons of the olive oil over medium heat. Add the shallots and the whites of the scallions and cook until soft and translucent, about 3 minutes. Pour in the broth, add the peas, and season with salt and pepper. Raise the heat to medium-high, bring to a boil, then reduce heat to low, cover, and simmer until the peas are tender, about 6 minutes.

Working in batches, transfer the soup to a blender or food processor and puree until smooth. Strain into a container, cover, and chill for 2 hours.

Taste and season the soup with salt and pepper as needed. In a small mixing bowl, toss the scallion greens with the remaining 2 tablespoons olive oil. When you are ready to serve, grill or toast the bread and spoon scallion greens over, place 1 crostino in each bowl, and divide the soup among the bowls. Sprinkle with mint chiffonade and serve.

BEET SALAD

with Baby Spinach and Goat Cheese

I fell in love with my wife over Coach Farm goat cheese when I first moved to New York City. It still makes me happy to cook with goat cheese, especially this simple salad where the beets' inherent sweetness makes the perfect foil for the creamy, tangy curds.

SERVES 6

2 large bunches beets, with greens

2 tablespoons extra-virgin olive oil

2 cups baby spinach, washed and spun dry

¼ cup Red Wine Vinaigrette (recipe below)

Kosher salt

8 ounces crumbly goat cheese, such as Coach Farm or La Tur

Preheat the oven to 400°F.

Cut off the beet greens, leaving ½ inch of the stem on each, and reserve them for ravioli filling or soups. Scrub the beets, toss them with the olive oil, and spread them in a baking pan. Roast until very tender, 50 to 60 minutes. Let cool slightly, then rub off the skins under running water and slice the stems into ⅛-inch pieces.

Cut the beets into ½-inch chunks and place them in a large bowl with the stem pieces. Add the spinach and toss with just enough vinaigrette to lightly coat. Season with salt.

Divide the salad among six plates, crumble some of the goat cheese over each salad, and serve.

RED WINE VINAIGRETTE

¼ cup red wine vinegar

1 tablespoon ice water

1 tablespoon grainy mustard

½ cup extra-virgin olive oil

Kosher salt and freshly ground black pepper

Whisk the vinegar, water, mustard, and olive oil together in a small bowl and season with salt and pepper. The vinaigrette can be stored in an airtight container in the refrigerator for up to 1 month.

MAKES 1 CUP

MOROCCAN CARROT SALAD

SERVES 6 TO 8

2 pounds carrots

½ cup extra-virgin olive oil

Zest and juice of 1 lemon

½ cup chopped fresh cilantro

4 cloves garlic, shredded on a
     Microplane

2 teaspoons ground cumin

1 teaspoon ground cinnamon

1 tablespoon sweet paprika

2 serrano chiles, finely chopped,
     with the seeds

Kosher salt and freshly ground
     black pepper

1 (4 ounce) tube or jar harissa or
     other hot sauce (optional)

One of my favorite things about travel in Morocco is the first course of cooked and raw salads served at almost every meal. This carrot salad is omnipresent: simple enough to be on my home table at least once a week and yet complicated enough in flavor to always surprise me.

Shred the carrots on the large holes of a box grater or in a food processor using a large-holed shredding disk.

Place the shredded carrots in a large bowl and add the oil, lemon zest, lemon juice, cilantro, garlic, cumin, cinnamon, paprika, and chiles and stir to mix well. Cover and let marinate in the refrigerator for at least 4 hours. Right before serving, season with salt and pepper. Serve chilled with a bowl of harissa or other hot sauce on the side, if desired.

FOCACCIA PANZANELLA

In Tuscany, bread salad has been a crafty use of leftover bread for generations. In the last twenty years, panzanella has become very hip in retro-gastronomic nostalgia, ruling the menus in trattorie in the Boot and the States. The trick is the super-tangy vinegar that dresses this whole madness so that the crunchy-crisp vegetables can really sing.

SERVES 6 TO 8

1 pound day-old focaccia, with crust, cut into ½-inch cubes (about 6 cups)

2 overripe large heirloom tomatoes (about 1½ pounds), cut into ½-inch dice

2 garden cucumbers, peeled, seeded, and cut into ½-inch half-moons

1 medium red onion, quartered and thinly sliced

½ cup extra-virgin olive oil

¼ cup red wine vinegar

Maldon salt and freshly ground black pepper

10 fresh basil leaves, torn

Combine the bread, tomatoes, cucumbers, and onion in a large serving bowl. Drizzle the olive oil and vinegar over the salad, stirring or tossing to mix well. Season well with sea salt and pepper and toss again. (The salad can be dressed up to 2 hours in advance and set aside at room temperature.)

Just before serving, tear the basil leaves and scatter them over the salad, then toss again.

Vail

Chef:
KELLY LIKEN, RESTAURANT KELLY LIKEN

Farmers:
MULTIPLE

Ingredients:
GOAT CHEESE, SWEET PEAS, CORN

It's noon on Sunday in early July. Kelly Liken's restaurant in Vail, Colorado, will be open in less than six hours.

There is no menu.

No one is panicking. On Sundays at this time of year, there's never a menu.

Her team of six chefs walks to the weekly outdoor market a block away. In an hour, they'll have procured ingredients and inspiration for a prix-fixe meal based on what they find.

Vail is a manicured ski town with a terrain ill suited to agriculture. But it's in the middle of the state, within reach of farming regions on both sides of the Rockies. A market takes over the pedestrian mall outside Kelly's restaurant on summer Sundays, and the chefs know where to find the farmers.

Kelly used to make low-key forays to the market in shorts and flip-flops and got to know the farmers. But Kelly's dad had an idea: Shop conspicuously. Get your team in their chef's jackets and go out en masse, talking about what you're buying and what you might make with it. It could generate interest in the restaurant and the farmers.

It worked.

The first stop is Miller Farms, a family farm about three hours away, near Denver. The Miller family has been farming since the 1940s and sells produce around the state.

Kelly has bought from the farm since she opened her restaurant. The stand is staffed by Miller kids, cousins, and in-laws, whom Kelly knows by name.

The chefs start shopping.

Andrew likes the pattypan squash and will make them part of a vegetarian entrée.

Sebastian sees a pile of corn and Anaheim peppers and wants to use them with his fish course. Kelly likes the idea, but wonders if the early season corn is sweet enough. She tries it, smiles, and hands the ear to Sebastian. He takes a bite and buys a dozen ears.

Colleen, the pastry chef, excitedly picks up a bag of English peas. Wait, for dessert?

The next stop is Jumpin' Good Goat Dairy, which makes goat cheeses in Buena Vista, ninety minutes south of Vail.

Dawn Jump designed her dairy and built it from the ground up—and from the ground down. The only place on the property from which you can't get a picturesque view of the surrounding mountains is in the caves she dug to age her cheese.

Dawn has as many as five hundred goats—all named—to give her the raw materials for the 300,000 pounds of cheese she makes each year.

Kelly likes the variety from Jumpin' Good. Cheesemaking is an art, and Dawn says limiting herself to the standards would be boring.

Tonight's menu will include a salad. The chefs sample First Snow, a rind-ripened cheese layered with vegetable ash. The name is cheeky: Gray ash against snow-white cheese evokes a winter's first snowfall discolored by pollution. Sold.

Andrew picks up some chèvre for the gnudi he's planning, to supplement the ricotta they have at the restaurant.

Any chefs not tasting cheese are discussing why Colleen bought peas.

The crew migrates to Eat a Peach. Jonathon Hieb used to be a chef but now helps run the farm, about two hours west of Vail.

In the late 1980s, Jonathon was working at a Texas restaurant called Sweet Pea, where he served the kind of food he now grows. He respects the parallel passions of people who work in kitchens and in fields.

It's too early in the season for Eat a Peach's namesake crop. Today the table is filled mostly with vegetables. Someone spots beets, so the salad is almost done.

Matt, Kelly's chef de cuisine, zeros in on beans. To be worthwhile for the restaurant, he'd have to buy them all. Matt knows that sometimes farmers don't like getting cleaned out, but Jonathon says it's fine. They go in the bag.

Kelly asks for a case of apricots, but Jonathon tells her they're a little early, and she might not want that many.

"It's okay, I'm going to pickle them," she says. "But thanks for telling me!"

Colleen heads to another booth to get honey and to avoid questions about dessert.

The last stop for the crew is Ripe, run by Gretchen Schramm and Mike Hovey. Ripe isn't a farm, but picks up produce from farms around the state to sell at markets and at their store, just west of Vail.

Kelly loads up on tomatoes for the week. She sees red torpedo onions and announces that someone should use them in something. A handful go into the bag.

Andrew wishes he had something green for his gnudi and squash dish. Someone points to a bunch of chard. Done.

Colleen has a big bag with red, yellow, orange, and purple carrots. And a big, big smile. Seems dessert is set, too.

Back in the kitchen, each cook tells Kelly his or her plan, and editing begins.

Andrew wants a curry custard with his gnudi dish. He and Kelly discuss the textures and the flavors. They test the custard and decide a cream sauce with those flavors is a better idea.

Sebastian pitches a plan for a corn and Anaheim salad to go with his fish course. Kelly likes the idea, but asks how hot the peppers are. They taste and decide to roast half and leave the rest raw, for contrast.

The give-and-take continues with the soup, the salad, the pork entrée. Kelly asks about dessert, and Colleen describes her plan for a brown-butter cake with pea-mint mousse, carrot sorbet, roasted carrots, and caramel. Kelly shoots Colleen a look that suggests she's just going to trust her.

When customers arrive a few hours later, here's what they get:

An amuse-bouche of wax bean and green bean slaw.

A roasted beet and apricot salad with goat cheese.

A choice of three entrées: pork with pickled peppers; skate wing with a salad of corn and chiles; or gnudi with roasted squash, sautéed chard, and curried cream.

A dessert called "Peas & Carrots" proves Kelly's trust was well placed.

It's an impressive result, but hardly the only possible one. With a shopping bag filled with peas, carrots, corn, tomatoes, peppers, beans, and cheese, anything is possible.

What would you have made?

GRILLED VEGETABLE SALAD

with Tomato Seed Vinaigrette

SERVES 6

Nothing makes me feel better than a main course salad (except maybe one served with a glass of wine…), and this is perhaps the most celebratory of all. I love grilling snow peas, and the radicchio makes the salad seem fancier than it really is.

FOR THE TOMATO SEED VINAIGRETTE

3 tablespoons sherry vinegar

1 tablespoon fresh thyme leaves

1 tablespoon mustard seeds

1 teaspoon red pepper flakes

2 overripe large heirloom tomatoes

½ cup extra-virgin olive oil

Kosher salt and freshly ground
    black pepper

FOR THE GRILLED VEGETABLES

2 red bell peppers, cored, seeded,
    and quartered

2 small yellow squash, cut lengthwise
    into ⅛-inch slices

2 heads Trevisano or Verona
    radicchio, quartered through
    the core

2 red onions, cut into ½-inch rounds

12 scallions, trimmed and cleaned

1 pound snow peas or sugar snap
    peas, trimmed and strings
    removed

Kosher salt

MAKE THE TOMATO SEED VINAIGRETTE

In a small bowl, whisk together the vinegar, thyme, mustard seeds, and red pepper flakes. Halve the tomatoes crosswise and gently but firmly squeeze out the seeds and juices into the bowl with the vinegar mixture—be sure to get most if not all of them. (Reserve the tomato flesh for a sandwich.) Whisk together, then continue whisking while you drizzle in the oil to form a viscous emulsion. Season with salt and pepper.

MAKE THE GRILLED VEGETABLES

Preheat a gas grill or prepare a fire in a charcoal grill.

Place the vegetables on three large baking sheets, keeping the snow peas separate from the others. Brush all the vegetables lightly with some of the vinaigrette and season lightly with salt. Place all the vegetables except the snow peas on the grill over medium-high heat and cook for 7 to 9 minutes until just lightly charred, and then turn and cook for 3 to 5 minutes more. Remove each vegetable from the grill as it is done and return to the baking sheets. Place a baking sheet with the snow peas on the grill and cook 2 minutes.

Arrange the vegetables, like the artist you are, on a large serving platter and drizzle with the remaining vinaigrette. Serve warm or at room temperature.

SPIGARELLO SALAD

with Spicy Currants and Fried Eggs

SERVES 6 TO 8

2 tablespoons dried currants

6 tablespoons white balsamic vinegar

2 tablespoons sriracha

6 tablespoons extra-virgin olive oil

Zest and juice of 1 lemon

1 tablespoon tiny capers, drained

1 teaspoon kosher salt, plus more as needed

2 bunches broccoli spigarello or Tuscan kale (about 1 pound), cut crosswise into paper-thin slices

2 tablespoons pine nuts, lightly toasted

6 to 8 large eggs (1 per person)

Freshly ground black pepper

¼ cup freshly grated Parmigiano-Reggiano

Adding eggs to a salad makes it more of a luxurious, substantive dish, and this salad is no exception. In Spain we often ate eggs as a main course for supper in restaurants. This recipe is a great way to try them as a main course at your house.

Place the currants in a small microwave-safe bowl; add the vinegar and sriracha and microwave for 20 seconds on high, then remove and place in a salad bowl to cool.

When cool, add 4 tablespoons of the olive oil, the lemon zest, lemon juice, capers, and salt and whisk together to form a light dressing.

Add the spigarello and toss with the vinaigrette to coat well. Add the pine nuts and let stand at room temperature for 10 minutes.

In a 10-inch nonstick pan, heat the remaining 2 tablespoons olive oil over medium heat.

Crack the eggs into the pan and cook slowly the way you like them—sunny-side up is best.

Season the eggs with salt and pepper and sprinkle the yolks with the Parmigiano.

Toss the salad one more time. Divide the salad among serving plates, slide an egg over the top of each, and serve.

FAST CAST-IRON-SKILLET NIÇOISE SALAD

SERVES 4

FOR THE VINAIGRETTE

1/3 cup sherry vinegar

2 tablespoons Dijon mustard

2/3 cup extra-virgin olive oil

Kosher salt and freshly ground
black pepper

FOR THE SALAD

2 tablespoons kosher salt, plus more
as needed

1/2 pound baby red potatoes, halved

4 large eggs

1/2 pound green beans, trimmed

2 tablespoons extra-virgin olive oil

1 pound tuna steak, cut into
4 (1-inch-thick) pieces

Freshly ground black pepper

2 cups arugula

1 cup pitted black olives

1 bunch radishes, trimmed and
sliced

12 anchovy fillets, rinsed

This salad is one of my favorite things, as it contains a few of my heroes: beans, tuna, anchovies, and eggs. I am also partial to the radishes, olives, spuds, and arugula. Maybe I am Niçoise myself, but this underlines a great point: Salads can have all of your favorite ingredients, so use a lot of them, but sparingly and in balance for harmony.

MAKE THE VINAIGRETTE

Combine the vinegar and mustard until smooth, then slowly whisk in the olive oil to create an emulsion. Season with salt and pepper. Set aside one-third of the vinaigrette to serve tableside in a little pitcher and place the remainder in a large bowl.

MAKE THE SALAD

Bring a 6-quart pot of water to a boil and add 2 tablespoons of salt. Add the potatoes and cook until tender but not falling apart, about 10 minutes. Remove the potatoes with a spider (leaving the water boiling) and let cool, then cut into 1/2-inch pieces. Set up an ice bath. Place the eggs in the boiling water and cook for 4 1/2 minutes, then transfer to the ice bath, let cool, and peel.

Set a 12-inch cast-iron skillet over high heat and get it very hot. Toss the beans with 1 tablespoon of the olive oil and put them in the pan, spreading them as flat as possible. Cook the beans without moving them for 2 minutes. Then cook, stirring the beans around as if for a stir-fry, for another minute. Transfer the beans to a plate and set aside.

Brush the tuna with the remaining 1 tablespoon oil and season with salt and pepper on both sides. Add the tuna to the skillet and cook for 2 to 3 minutes on each side, until rare. Transfer to a plate and let rest.

Slice the tuna into 1/4-inch-thick slices. Cut the boiled eggs in half and sprinkle the yolks with coarse salt and set aside.

Place the cooked potatoes, beans, arugula, and olives in the bowl with the vinaigrette and toss gently to coat. Lay the vegetable mixture on a nice platter, arrange the tuna, radishes, salted eggs, and anchovy fillets over the top, and serve.

APPLE SALAD

with Salami and Wine-Marinated Mushrooms

I love a salad with crunchy sweet apples. The earthy addition of mushrooms in the vinaigrette really takes this salad to a different field of flavor. You can substitute any cured meat for the finocchiona, but make sure you get it from my dad's Salumi Artisan Cured Meats.

SERVES 4

FOR THE MARINATED MUSHROOMS

½ pound cremini mushrooms

½ pound shiitake mushrooms

1 cup dry red wine

¼ cup red wine vinegar

6 cups water

2 tablespoons whole black peppercorns

2 tablespoons kosher salt

1 sprig fresh rosemary

Pinch of red pepper flakes

FOR THE APPLE SALAD

1 Ginger Gold apple, or another tart apple, such as Granny Smith, peeled and cored

1 small head radicchio

¼ teaspoon caraway seeds

¼ cup red wine vinegar

1 teaspoon kosher salt

Freshly ground black pepper

¼ pound finocchiona (from my dad) or any firm salami, cut into julienne

¼ cup extra-virgin olive oil

MAKE THE MUSHROOMS

Clean any dirt from the mushrooms with a brush; do not wash them. Halve the creminis and remove the tough stems from the shiitakes. Break or cut the shiitakes into 1-inch pieces.

Pour the wine and vinegar into an 8-quart saucepan and add the water, peppercorns, and the salt. Bring to a boil.

Add the rosemary sprig to the pot. Then add the mushrooms all at once (leave any loose bits on the cutting board). Add the red pepper flakes and stir. Return the mixture to a boil, then reduce the heat to maintain a simmer, cover, and cook for 20 minutes.

Ladle the mushrooms into storage containers, top off with the cooking liquid, and let cool. (These mushrooms will store well in the fridge for up to 1 week. If you want to can them for longer storage, go to usda.gov and search for "canning.")

MAKE THE APPLE SALAD

When you are ready to assemble the salad, drain 1½ cups of the marinated mushrooms and place them in a salad bowl.

Cut the apple into ⅛-inch julienne and toss it in with the mushrooms.

Add the radicchio, caraway, vinegar, salt, and pepper to taste. Add the salami pieces and olive oil, toss well to mix, and serve.

Four:
SANDWICHES

TOMATO FOCACCIA

Rich with toasty yeast flavor and fragrant with tomato harvest sweetness, this is a simple bread you can make in a home oven that may be better than at the local bakery. If for some reason you have leftover bread, the panzanella recipe on page 94 can help you use it up in a tasty way.

MAKES TWO 11-BY-17-INCH FOCACCIA

1½ cups warm water, 105° to 115°F

1 (¼-ounce) package active dry yeast (2½ teaspoons)

3 tablespoons kosher salt

1 tablespoon honey

4 cups high-gluten pizza or bread flour, plus more for dusting

¾ cup extra-virgin olive oil, plus more as needed

6 ripe heirloom tomatoes, cut into ½-inch-thick slices

1 tablespoon coarse sea salt

Put the warm water in a large warmed bowl, add the yeast, and stir to dissolve. Let stand for 3 minutes, or until foamy.

Add 1 tablespoon of the kosher salt and the honey and stir to combine. Add the flour and ½ cup of the oil and mix, first with the spoon and then using your hands, until the dough comes together into a slightly tacky ball.

Wash and dry your hands. Transfer the dough to a floured work surface and knead, occasionally dusting it with a teaspoon of flour at a time, until you form a smooth, firm, homogeneous ball, about 15 minutes. (You can do this just as well in a stand mixer fitted with a dough hook if you are in a hurry, but consider doing it by hand. It makes you a better person.)

Place the dough in a lightly oiled large bowl and cover it with a clean kitchen cloth. Place the bowl in a warm area (such as on the stove) and let rise until the dough has doubled in size, about 1 hour.

Punch down the dough and divide it into 2 equal pieces. Shape each one into a ball, return to the bowl, cover, and let rise for 30 minutes.

Preheat the oven to 450°F. Lightly oil two 11-by-17-inch baking sheets, the older the better.

Place a dough ball on each of the oiled baking sheets and, using your fingertips, poke indentations across the entire surface of the dough, spreading the dough out over the sheet. Let them rise in a warm place for 30 minutes. Sprinkle each with 1 tablespoon of the kosher salt, drizzle with some of the remaining olive oil, and then lay the tomato slices on top, barely overlapping, like shingles, to cover to within ½ inch of the edge of the dough. Drizzle the remaining oil over to form slight puddles in some of the dimples, and sprinkle with the sea salt. Bake for 14 to 15 minutes until golden brown on top and bottom. Serve warm.

PEPERONATA WITH BRUSCHETTA

The Italian way with sweet peppers starts with this basic sweet pepper stew, emboldened by the jalapeños, seasoned with the anchovies, and yet smooth and tangy as both of those players become background singers in the final presentation.

MAKES 6 BRUSCHETTA

3 tablespoons extra-virgin olive oil

1 red onion, cut into julienne

2 red bell peppers, cored, seeded, and cut into thin strips

2 yellow bell peppers, cored, seeded, and cut into thin strips

2 jalapeños, seeded and thinly sliced

2 anchovy fillets, rinsed and chopped

2 tablespoons sherry vinegar

Kosher salt and freshly ground black pepper

1 teaspoon fresh marjoram leaves

6 (1-inch-thick) slices filone or any good crusty bread

4 cloves garlic

In a 12- to 14-inch sauté pan, heat the olive oil over high heat until almost smoking. Add the onion, bell peppers, jalapeños, and anchovy fillets and sauté over high heat for 4 minutes, or until browned at the edges and softened. Add the sherry vinegar and salt and black pepper to taste, reduce the heat to medium, and continue to cook for 5 to 7 minutes more, until the peppers are tender. Season with salt and black pepper if needed and set aside to cool, then add the marjoram and stir.

Grill or toast the bread, turning it once, until marked with grill marks or deep golden brown but still soft in the center. Rub a garlic clove just around the circumference of each piece of toast, along the jagged outer crust. Arrange the toast on a serving platter. Spoon 2 or 3 tablespoons of the peperonata over the toast and serve warm.

ARUGULA AND FONTINA PANINO

with Cayenne-Maple Mustard

SERVES 4

½ cup brown deli mustard

¼ cup grade B maple syrup

2 teaspoons ground cayenne

2 teaspoons celery seeds

3 tablespoons extra-virgin olive oil

1 medium onion, cut into ¼-inch dice

4 bunches arugula, cleaned and spun dry (keep 1 bunch separate and roughly chop the other 3 bunches)

Maldon salt and freshly cracked black pepper

8 slices whole-grain bread

8 ounces grated Fontina Val d'Aosta (or substitute great American cheddar)

4 tablespoons (½ stick) unsalted butter

I hijacked this idea from Daphne Oz's Grilled Cheese in Relish. When she cooked it on The Chew *with roasted cauliflower, I subbed in the hammered braised greens.*

Preheat the oven to 250°F.

Combine the mustard, maple syrup, cayenne, and celery seeds in a small bowl and set aside.

In a 10- to 12-inch nonstick pan, heat the oil over medium heat. Add the onion and cook until just lightly golden brown, 5 to 6 minutes.

Add three-quarters of the chopped arugula and cook for 5 to 6 minutes, until completely wilted, then remove from the pan, season with salt and pepper, and set aside. Wipe out the pan with a paper towel and set it back over medium-low heat.

Spread 8 slices of bread with the mustard mixture; reserve the remaining mustard mixture for serving. Divide the braised arugula among 4 slices of the bread and flatten it a bit to make it even to the crust, then divide the grated cheese and the remaining raw arugula among the slices and top each with a second slice of bread.

Melt 2 tablespoons of the butter in the pan. Add two of the sandwiches, with the cheese side closer to the heat source, and cook for 4 to 6 minutes, until the bottom is golden and the cheese begins to melt. Gently press the top of the sandwich. Flip the sandwiches and cook the other side for 3 to 4 minutes. Transfer to a heatproof platter and keep warm in the oven while you toast the remaining two sandwiches in the remaining 2 tablespoons butter.

Cut each sandwich in half and serve warm, with the extra mustard on the side.

San Francisco

Chef:
BRUCE HILL, RESTAURANT PICCO

Farmer:
ANDY GRIFFIN, MARIQUITA FARM

Ingredient:
PEPPERS

Bruce Hill looks forward to Padrón pepper season. At his restaurants around San Francisco, you can find them sliced into rings on top of a white pizza with mortadella.

Or stuffed with poached tuna. Or roasted and turned into a relish. Or just fried and salted.

If he used to think they were expensive, that changed when he went to Mariquita Farm in Watsonville, California, to get a firsthand look at the fields where his favorite peppers grow.

Andy Griffin, the farmer at Mariquita, was happy to show him around.

It would have been easy to tell Bruce the numbers involved in the cost of picking the peppers. Bruce probably would have accepted it and moved on. But Andy told Bruce to go pick a pound of Padróns. He didn't tell him he was watching the clock.

The chef came back with a pound of peppers, blistered them over a fire in the field where they were harvested, salted them, and scarfed them down. Then Andy told him how long it had taken to pick them. He reminded Bruce how much Padróns cost per pound. Then he did the math: If his workers took as long to harvest a pound of peppers as Bruce did, Andy couldn't pay them minimum wage.

You aren't paying for the produce, he told Bruce. You're paying for the labor.

* * *

Andy says that he didn't take up farming after a successful career in IT, and that his career as a male model never worked out.

But before he started Mariquita, he did the agricultural equivalent of posing for the cover of *GQ*: He worked in the garden that supplied Chez Panisse in Berkeley. Does it get any sexier than growing vegetables for Alice Waters?

Andy used to sell at the high-profile farmers' markets in the area, but he doesn't anymore. He doesn't need to. His farm supplies about fifty restaurants around San Francisco and runs a CSA. The restaurants and the CSA families are divergent customer bases, a dichotomy Andy appreciates.

Restaurants call the shots on what they want. They need to impress diners. Andy has a field of nasturtiums that he grows for a restaurant that makes a soup with the flowers. He grows sorrel because every French restaurant on his list wants it.

The CSA customers want the basics. They need to feed the family. They get tomatoes, peppers, squash, potatoes. They don't get nasturtium flowers. They wouldn't want them.

* * *

It's eight in the morning and Andy is sitting outside the packing house at Mariquita. He's on the phone with his crews in the field.

Spanish isn't Andy's native language, but he's picked it up over the years. He would be able to communicate with his workers in English, but by learning Spanish, he has a better handle on what's going on around him and can become part of the social fabric of the people he counts on.

You don't have to speak Spanish to have a feel for how this phone call is going. Each sentence seems similarly punctuated:

"*Excelente!*"

"*Muy bien!*"

"*Perfecto!*"

"*Muchas gracias!*"

"*Exactamente!*"

Sounds like everything is going well this morning.

The nature of nature leads to a migratory working class on farms. When a farm specializes in growing one thing, there's a lot of work for a while, then none. The more specialized the farm, the less sustained the work.

So the farmer hires as many workers as he can or needs, brings in his crop, then says *gracias* and *hasta la vista* until next time. Workers move to the next farm with a crop ready to go.

The model is relatively inexpensive for the farmer but has problems for both sides: The workers can't become a part of a community. Their kids are uprooted to follow the harvest from one region to the next. Farmers spend time every season teaching a group of workers the same things a different group was taught last year. And they'll do it again next year. Consistency is impossible.

And competition is cutthroat. Even if a farmer secures workers, another farmer could lure them away by offering a few more pennies. Crops can die in the field. It's a cycle of inefficiency.

Andy thought if he could turn his farm into a year-round operation, he could keep a core crew on the job and it would make everyone's life better.

If he's there for them, they'll be there for him. Idealistic, maybe. But then it pays off.

One Saturday, Andy and his crew planted thousands of mixed greens seedlings. As they finished, they found that the piece that connected the irrigation system to the supply was broken, meaning there was no way to water the plants.

The irrigation supply store was closed for the weekend. By the time the store opened Monday it could be too late. Not only would Andy lose all the money invested in the seedlings, but he'd never make the money that the crop would have brought.

It was a certifiable disaster.

But while Andy was mentally calculating his losses, two of his employees were solving the problem. No one asked them to. They did it because they knew how, because they were invested. Without those greens to tend, pick, and sell, they stood to lose, too.

They started a small fire and heated the plastic tubing until it became malleable enough to force into the supply line. It held. They made it look easy. Before Andy could finish tallying his potential loss, there wasn't one anymore.

Andy is an equal-opportunity educator. He has a corollary to the economics lesson he gave Bruce.

One day, he and some other farmers were discussing restaurant prices. The farmers were calculating the markup for a salad, and they weren't happy about it. Andy gave them things to think about.

Did you factor in the salary of the chef who put it together? The salary of the server? The guy who washes the dishes? Those all have to show up in the cost of the food.

You aren't paying for the produce, he essentially told them. You're paying for the labor.

CAPONATA "SUBS"

SERVES 4

¼ cup extra-virgin olive oil, plus more as needed

2 cloves garlic, halved

1 large Spanish onion, cut into ½-inch dice

2 ribs celery, cut into thin ¼-inch slices

2 teaspoons chopped fresh thyme

2 medium eggplant, cut into ½-inch cubes (about 4 cups)

Kosher salt

1 (6-ounce) can tomato paste

¼ cup dried currants

¼ cup pine nuts

1 teaspoon ground cinnamon

1 teaspoon unsweetened cocoa powder

1 tablespoon red pepper flakes

2 tablespoons red wine vinegar

2 teaspoons sugar

Freshly ground black pepper

¼ cup water

1 baguette, cut into 4 pieces, split open to stuff

¼ cup freshly grated Pecorino Romano

¼ pound provolone, grated

I have eaten many eggplant Parmigiana over the years in New Jersey and in Little Italy, but this caponata variation is easier, lighter, more delicious, and just plain less messy to make. Unused caponata becomes tomorrow's lunch or tonight's antipasto in a flash.

Preheat the oven to 375°F.

In a 12- to 14-inch sauté pan, heat the olive oil over medium-high heat until almost smoking. Add the garlic, onion, celery, thyme, eggplant, and a couple of pinches of salt. Stir together, reduce the heat to medium, and cook for 5 to 6 minutes, or until the eggplant turns golden. If it looks a little dry, add 1 tablespoon of oil.

Add the tomato paste, currants, pine nuts, cinnamon, cocoa powder, and red pepper flakes and continue to cook for 3 minutes more.

Add the vinegar and allow it to evaporate. Add the sugar, salt and pepper to taste, and water and cook for 5 minutes more, then remove from the heat.

Place the baguette pieces in the oven to toast until golden. Remove and stuff each baguette piece with about ½ cup of the caponata and top with Pecorino Romano and provolone. Place the stuffed bread on a baking sheet and return it to the oven. Bake until the cheese is nicely melted. Remove and serve immediately.

SAUSAGE AND PEPPER "HEROS"

SERVES 4

¼ cup extra-virgin olive oil

4 links fresh hot or sweet Italian sausages

1 medium red onion, cut into ¼-inch dice

2 red bell peppers, seeded and cut into ½-inch dice

2 yellow bell peppers, seeded and cut into ½-inch dice

1 teaspoon red pepper flakes

4 salt-packed anchovy fillets, rinsed and chopped

2 tablespoons fresh thyme leaves

1 (6-ounce) can tomato paste

½ cup dry red wine

Best-quality long sub roll or baguette

½ cup freshly grated Parmigiano-Reggiano

½ pound best-quality mozzarella, thinly sliced

These will be only as good as the sausages and bread you use to make them, so head to the best Italian butcher in your town and get the hottest homemade sausages you can stand and make sure there are fennel seeds in them, too; it is the difference between success and anonymity. Same story for the bread; crusty loaves will distinguish you from your slacker neighbors.

In a 12- to 14-inch sauté pan, heat the olive oil over medium heat. Add the sausages and cook until they are browned, 4 to 5 minutes on each side. Set aside on a plate. Add the onion, bell peppers, red pepper flakes, anchovies, and thyme to the pan and cook, stirring regularly, until the vegetables are soft, about 10 minutes.

Add the tomato paste and wine and bring to a boil. Return the sausages to the pan, reduce the heat to maintain a simmer, and cook for about 5 minutes, then flip the sausages and cook for 10 minutes more. At this point, you can hold the mixture on the stovetop for up to 2 hours.

An hour before you want to eat, preheat the oven to 325°F.

Cut the sub roll/baguette into 4-inch pieces and split them, with the back side attached to hold the sauce. Place a sausage and 2 tablespoons of the pepper mixture into each piece. Sprinkle with 1 tablespoon of Parmigiano and add 2 slices of mozzarella to each. Individually wrap the subs loosely in foil. Place the assembled subs in the oven for 40 minutes, or until ready to eat. Even an hour later, they will be great.

GREEN TOMATO "FOLDERS"

with Prosciutto and Caprino

MAKES 8 PIECES

2 large green tomatoes

4 ounces fresh caprino (goat cheese), crumbled

8 slices prosciutto

8 fresh sage leaves

1½ cups all-purpose flour

1 tablespoon kosher salt

2 large eggs

¼ cup whole milk

2 cups panko bread crumbs

1 tablespoon freshly cracked black pepper

6 tablespoons extra-virgin olive oil

1 lemon, cut into wedges

These little packets are inspired by the Southern pimento cheese–wearing variety and have a creamy ham-y filling that makes them almost a main course.

Cut each green tomato crosswise into 8 thin slices and lay them out on a work surface. Sprinkle 8 of the slices with the crumbled goat cheese. Over the cheese, place 1 piece of prosciutto, folded to fit. Place 1 sage leaf on top and cover with a second tomato slice. Press down lightly with your fingers to compress somewhat.

Set up a breading station. Place the flour in a shallow bowl and season with the salt. Place the eggs and milk in a second bowl and beat together lightly. Place the panko in a third bowl and season with the pepper.

Dredge each tomato "folder" first in the flour, then in the egg-milk mixture, then in the panko, pressing firmly to help it adhere, and set aside.

Preheat the oven to 225°F.

In a large nonstick skillet, heat 4 tablespoons of the olive oil over medium heat until just smoking. Place 4 "folders" in the pan and cook until golden brown, about 3 minutes. Turn over carefully and cook until the second side is golden brown and the cheese is soft and melted. Transfer to a plate and keep warm in the oven. Add the remaining 2 tablespoons of oil to the pan and fry the remaining "folders."

Serve warm with lemon wedges.

LAMB SHANK SLOPPY JOES

with Onion Marmalade

I have no problem serving gussied-up sandwiches at a dinner party, provided there is spectacular flavor and texture. The gelatinous and succulent meat combined with a perfectly toasted bun and red onion marmalade fits the bill to a T and can carry a fancy wine, if you like to enjoy the sacred and the profane as I do.

SERVES 6

FOR THE MARMALADE

2 medium red onions, cut into ¼-inch dice

2 cups Lambrusco or other light-bodied fruity red wine

1 cup orange juice

½ cup sugar

2 juniper berries

FOR THE LAMB SHANK RAGU

3 tablespoons extra-virgin olive oil

2 pounds lamb shank meat (from 3 lamb shanks), cut into 1-inch cubes

Kosher salt and freshly ground black pepper

1 large Spanish onion, cut into ¼-inch dice

6 cloves garlic, thinly sliced

1 small carrot, cut into ¼-inch dice

1 rib celery, cut into ¼-inch dice

1 cup dry white wine

1 (28-ounce) can whole Italian plum tomatoes, crushed, with their juices

TO ASSEMBLE

6 firm ciabatta or kaiser rolls

1 tablespoon fresh rosemary leaves, chopped

2 bunches watercress

MAKE THE MARMALADE

In a 2-quart saucepan, combine the red onions, Lambrusco, orange juice, sugar, and juniper berries. Set over high heat and bring to a boil. Lower the heat to medium and reduce until thick like a marmalade, about 60 minutes. Remove from the heat and let cool. Remove the juniper berries and set aside.

MAKE THE LAMB SHANK RAGU

In a heavy-bottomed pot, heat the olive oil over medium-high heat until smoking. Season the lamb pieces with salt and pepper and cook until deep, dark, golden brown on all sides, about 15 minutes. Add the onion, garlic, carrot, and celery and cook until slightly caramelized and light golden brown, 10 to 12 minutes. Add the wine and tomatoes and bring to a boil. Reduce the heat to maintain a simmer and cook for 90 minutes, or until the lamb is fork-tender. Shred the lamb pieces with two forks and set aside to cool in the refrigerator overnight so the flavors will marry and the ragu will develop more complexity.

ASSEMBLE THE DISH

Slice the breads in half lengthwise and grill or toast them. In a medium saucepan, reheat the ragu over low heat until piping hot. On the top half of the bread, spread the onion marmalade and sprinkle with the rosemary. Spoon the lamb onto the bottom half, making sure to overfill the sandwich with the stuffing. Garnish the sloppy joes with a good fistful of the watercress and serve.

Five:
PASTA

FETTUCCINE

with My Grandma's Sparerib Sauce

SERVES 4 TO 6

¼ cup extra-virgin olive oil

4 pounds pork spareribs, cut into 2-inch pieces

2 medium red onions, cut into ¼-inch dice

2 carrots, cut into ½-inch pieces

2 salt-packed anchovy fillets, rinsed and patted dry

1 (6-ounce) can tomato paste

1 cup dry white wine

3 cups Basic Tomato Sauce (page 145)

1 sprig fresh rosemary

3 tablespoons kosher salt

1 (1-pound) package fettuccine

1 cup freshly grated Parmigiano-Reggiano

We always thought it was a little strange that Grandma Batali served meat with bones in it with the pasta, but we never, ever questioned the unbelievable depth of flavor that these tasty little ribs brought to the table at her house on Sundays. The flavor is haunting and the texture superb.

In a large Dutch oven, heat the olive oil over medium heat until smoking. Add the spareribs, 6 or 7 pieces at a time, and cook until deep golden brown on all sides, 8 to 10 minutes per batch. Transfer each batch to a bowl and repeat with the remaining spareribs. Add the onions, carrots, anchovies, and the tomato paste to the pan and cook for 6 minutes, or until it takes on a rusty color. Add the wine and tomato sauce and stir to dislodge all the browned bits from the bottom of the pan. Cover and bring to a boil. Add the rosemary sprig and the browned ribs to the bubbling sauce, reduce the heat to maintain a simmer, cover, and cook until the ribs are fork-tender, about 1½ hours.

When ready to eat, bring 8 quarts of water to a boil in a pasta pot and add the salt. Remove the ribs from the Dutch oven and place them on a plate. Drop the pasta into the boiling water and cook it for 1 minute less than directed on the package. Drain in a colander and add to the pan with the sauce. Toss over medium heat to coat and dress the pasta. Pour the pasta and sauce into a heated serving bowl, arrange the ribs over the top, and serve immediately with the Parmigiano-Reggiano on the side.

SPAGHETTI

with Spicy Almond Pesto

SERVES 4 TO 6;
MAKES 1½ CUPS PESTO

1 cup lightly packed fresh basil leaves, washed and spun dry

½ cup fresh mint leaves, washed and spun dry

3 cloves garlic

2 serrano chiles, stems removed

1 teaspoon red pepper flakes

1 teaspoon fennel seeds

1 cup sliced blanched almonds

½ cup extra-virgin olive oil, plus ¼ cup if needed

¼ cup freshly grated Pecorino Siciliano, plus more for serving

2 tablespoons kosher salt, plus more as needed

1 (1-pound) package spaghetti

This spicy pesto has the basil we all recognize, but then speeds off the tracks with serranos, fennel seeds, and almonds for an exotic ride into the markets of Palermo, where this dish was born. Adjust the heat to your taste; it is quite spicy in my house.

Place the basil, mint, garlic, chiles, red pepper flakes, fennel seeds, and almonds in a food processor and pulse 3 times to roughly chop. Add ½ cup of the oil and pulse 4 or 5 times to create a thick paste (not a thin, oily sauce). Add ¼ cup of the Pecorino Siciliano and pulse once to combine. Taste and season with salt if it needs it. If not using immediately, transfer to a container with a lid. Carefully pour ¼ cup more olive oil over the pesto to seal out air, cover with a tight lid, and refrigerate. The pesto can be stored in the fridge for 2 weeks.

Bring 8 quarts of water to boil in a pasta pot and add the salt.

Place 1 cup of the pesto in a large warmed bowl.

Drop the spaghetti into the boiling water and cook it for 1 minute less than directed on the package. Just before it is done, carefully ladle ¼ cup of the cooking water into the bowl with the pesto. Drain the pasta in a colander and dump it into the bowl with the pesto and the cooking water. Toss gently like a salad for about 30 seconds, until nicely coated, and serve with a scant dusting of cheese over each portion.

SPAGHETTI

with Jalapeño-Walnut Pesto

Rich, oily, and fragrant, this pesto makes a great pasta sauce, but also a superb accompaniment to a cheese plate as well as an excellent sandwich condiment. So go ahead, make a double batch.

SERVES 4 TO 6

8 jalapeños, stems removed, seeds intact

1 cup walnut pieces

½ red onion, diced

½ cup extra-virgin olive oil

3 tablespoons kosher salt

1 (1-pound) package thick spaghetti

Toasted almond slivers (optional)

2 teaspoons chipotle powder

Preheat the oven to 450°F.

Combine the jalapeños, the walnuts, and the onion in the bowl of a food processor. Pulse until pureed, then slowly drizzle in the oil until emulsified. (The jalapeño pesto can be stored in an airtight container in the refrigerator for up to 2 weeks.)

Bring 8 quarts of water to a boil in a pasta pot and add the salt. Place 1 cup jalapeño pesto in a large, warmed bowl.

Drop the spaghetti into the boiling water and cook for 1 minute less than directed on the package. Just before the pasta is done, carefully ladle ¼ cup of the cooking water into the bowl with the pesto. Drain the pasta well in a colander and toss into the bowl with the pesto. Toss like a salad until well coated. Sprinkle with toasted almond slivers, if desired, and the chipotle powder and serve immediately.

Seattle

Chef:
MATT DILLON, THE CORSON BUILDING

Farmer:
PIERRE MONNAT, OLD CHASER FARM

Ingredients:
LAMB, FAVA BEANS

Pierre Monnat has his hands in a little bit of everything.

Right now, they're wrist-deep in dirt, digging holes to plant lettuce seedlings.

Looking around the half-acre of cultivated space at Old Chaser Farm on Vashon Island, just off the coast of Seattle, you see a lot of things growing.

Without taking a step, you can see lettuce, beets, onions, peas, fava beans, kale, radicchio, zucchini, carrots, fennel, cabbage, chard, sunchokes, tomatoes, and peppers. That doesn't include the fruit trees.

Pierre wishes there were a little more diversity.

A week ago, the rows Pierre is working were filled with heads of lettuce that were harvested for customers of the farm's CSA. Today, he tilled the patch, and now he's breaking seedlings off a tray that he started in the greenhouse three weeks ago. In a fluid motion, he plunges his hand into the dirt, drops a root ball into the hole he created, pats the soil, and starts over. In just a couple of minutes, six dozen heads of green lettuce are in the ground. In about a month, they'll be harvested. He repeats the process with red lettuce. Then with two dozen cucumber plants. Then he direct-sows three rows of turnip seeds.

It hasn't been an hour and the patch of dark, empty earth has been filled with four crops.

He picks up another tray of seedlings and walks to the garden, where he stops and looks around. He realizes he has nowhere to plant them. Something is growing everywhere. Then, obscured behind a robust row of leafy chard, he sees two rows where he harvested this morning. He breaks out the tiller to get it ready.

"I love growing vegetables. I want to do it for the rest of my life."

Matt Dillon, the chef-owner of a handful of high-quality restaurants in Seattle, brings an independent spirit to his ventures, developed honestly from spending his formative years playing in a punk rock band. He and some partners bought Old Chaser Farm because he liked the idea of making his restaurants more self-sufficient. Given the choice and the chance, he'd rather grow something than buy it.

Pierre is a childhood acquaintance who reconnected with Matt after going to Matt's restaurant Sitka & Spruce. Soon after, Matt was looking for someone to run operations at Old Chaser and remembered Pierre.

Pierre tends the garden and cares for the farm's livestock, which include sheep, pigs, goats, and the occasional cow, most of which are destined for Matt's restaurants.

Working hard and efficiently is a hallmark of employees in the restaurants, so Pierre's ability to tear through a to-do list makes him a perfect fit.

Matt estimates that the farm is a one-and-a-half-person job. He counts himself as the half to Pierre's one.

But, Matt admits, Pierre might do the work of more than one person.

The plan for Old Chaser to supply Matt's restaurants had a problem: It meant giving up relationships with all the other farmers Matt helped support. So he developed a Plan B. Instead, the farm would start a CSA, but one unlike the average box of vegetables. Sure, there would be Pierre's produce. But the restaurants get in on the act, too, supplying bread, dairy products, jams, jellies, and pickles. And for good measure, Matt's team picks a wine that complements the week's other items and adds that, too.

With just a little bit of imagination, it's dinner.

For those without imagination, they throw in recipes.

Matt isn't the only help Pierre has at the farm. He also has his rottweilers, Lemmy and Opie. In theory, they could help a lot. They could be, say, guard dogs. They present an intimidating first impression. But the dogs have a secret: A handful of treats will buy their silence.

Historically, rottweilers are herding dogs. So maybe they could help out with the livestock? Pierre brought Lemmy into the field with the sheep once, and Lemmy saw a lamb that he thought he could exert some authority over. What Lemmy didn't see was the lamb's mother.

The ewe interceded, and Lemmy held his ground, but with a diminishing sense of confidence. Then the ewe head-butted Lemmy, sending him running away with his tail between his legs. Literally.

Whatever shepherding instinct rottweilers had has been bred out, Pierre concluded.

So Lemmy mostly hangs out in the vegetable patch now, keeping the fava beans in line.

Pierre's efficiency gives him time to pick up hobbies. He mills fallen trees and uses the lumber in the woodworking shed he set up at the farm. He dabbles in forestry management and has drawn up plans on how the trees on the property could be maintained.

He shears sheep for neighbors on the island. He trims the hooves of neighbors' goats.

He makes time for those things because he finds them fun and fulfilling. (Well, not trimming goats' hooves. He does that for the money.)

Pierre has an understated, exceedingly thoughtful, matter-of-fact manner. But he gets excited talking about a new plant he just got: hops.

The main reason is that he likes vining plants. Seriously, that's the main reason.

It's also, in part, because he likes beer. He can trace the lineage of craft brewers in the area, pointing out which beers are brewed where, which have moved out of the area, and which has been his favorite since he was fifteen.

Revealing that, he looks up with a sly smile, as if he just slipped but knows there's nothing you can do about it.

So he's a beer lover. He's growing hops. And he picks up hobbies like they were cash on the sidewalk. He's making his own beer, right?

Nah, it's too easy to pick up a six-pack. He says he's unlikely to make better beer than he could buy. And if he couldn't make it better, it would frustrate him.

So no brewing yet. But who knows. One day, he might make time to try.

ORECCHIETTE
with Sausage and Collards

SERVES 4 TO 6

FOR THE PASTA

2 cups semolina flour, plus more for sprinkling

2 cups all-purpose flour, plus more for dusting

1 to 1¼ cups warm water

FOR THE RAGU

5 tablespoons extra-virgin olive oil

1½ pounds Italian pork sausage, casings removed

1 red onion, cut into ¼-inch dice

1 rib celery, cut into ½-inch dice

Kosher salt and freshly ground black pepper

1 (6-ounce) can tomato paste

1 cup water

4 cloves garlic, thinly sliced

1 teaspoon red pepper flakes (optional)

1 large bunch collard greens, tough stems trimmed

TO ASSEMBLE

3 tablespoons kosher salt

Pecorino Toscano, for serving

The incredible chewy texture of this homemade pasta is easy to achieve; the trick is the warm water and the kneading time. We often spend a Sunday morning with the kids and make a triple batch; orecchiette freeze well and hold indefinitely, and besides that, they are a lot of fun to make.

MAKE THE PASTA

Place both flours in a large bowl and stir to combine well. Make a well in the center of the flour mixture and add the water a little at a time, stirring with your hands, until a dough is formed. You may need more or less water, depending on the humidity in your kitchen.

Place the dough on a floured work surface and knead it like bread dough for 8 to 10 minutes, until smooth and elastic. Cover and let stand for 10 minutes at room temperature.

Roll the dough into long dowels about ¾ inch thick. Cut the dowels into flat disks about ¼ inch to ½ inch thick. Press the center of each disk with your thumb to form saucer-shaped pasta, and place the orecchiette on a baking sheet that has been sprinkled with semolina. Cover with a clean dish towel and set aside.

MAKE THE RAGU

In a large skillet or Dutch oven, heat 2 tablespoons of the olive oil over high heat. Place the sausage in the pan and cook until the fat has rendered, moving the sausage occasionally to avoid sticking. Remove the meat and set aside. Drain the excess fat from the pan, reduce the heat to low, and add the onion and celery. Season with salt and pepper, and sweat the vegetables for about 6 minutes, until tender, letting them get soft but not browned. Add the tomato paste and 1 cup water, bring the mixture to a boil, and return the sausage to the pan. Reduce the heat to maintain a simmer and cook for 20 to 30 minutes, until the mixture has a ragu consistency. Add more water, if necessary, to keep the ragu moist.

Continued on page 142.

In a 12- to 14-inch sauté pan, heat the remaining 3 tablespoons olive oil over high heat until almost smoking. Add the garlic, red pepper flakes, and collards and toss until the collards are tender, about 10 minutes. Add the ragu and toss for 2 minutes, seasoning with salt and black pepper as needed.

ASSEMBLE THE DISH

Bring 8 quarts of water to a boil in a pasta pot and add the salt. Drop the orecchiette into the boiling water and cook until tender yet al dente, about 6 minutes. Drain the pasta and add it to the pan with the collards and ragu. Toss over medium heat for 1 minute, then divide the pasta and sauce evenly among six warm pasta bowls. Grate Pecorino Toscano over each bowl and serve immediately.

POTATO GNOCCHI

al Pomodoro

Comfort food, Batali family–style. These are the gateway pasta that will lead to a lifelong addiction to making your own pasta at home.

SERVES 4 TO 6

3 pounds starchy russet potatoes

2 cups all-purpose flour, plus more for dusting

1 extra-large egg

¼ cup extra-virgin olive oil

2 tablespoons kosher salt, plus more as needed

2 cups Basic Tomato Sauce (page 145)

12 fresh basil leaves

Place the potatoes in a large saucepan and add cool water to cover. Bring the water to a boil and cook the potatoes until soft, about 45 minutes. While still warm, peel the potatoes and pass them through a food mill onto a clean pasta board.

Bring 6 quarts of water to a boil in a large pot. Set up an ice bath next to the stovetop with 4 cups of ice and 3 quarts of water.

Make a well in the center of the potatoes and sprinkle them with the flour. Place the egg and a pinch of salt in the center of the well and, using a fork, stir the egg into the flour and potatoes. Bring the dough together, kneading gently until a ball is formed. Continue to knead gently for 4 minutes more, or until the dough is dry to the touch. Cut a tennis ball–size hunk of dough off the main ball and roll it into a dowel about ¾ inch thick.

Cut across the dowel to form lozenges about 1 inch long. Roll each down the tines of a fork to form the traditional gnocchi shape. Repeat with the remaining dough. Keep the formed gnocchi on a lightly floured baking sheet.

Drop a third of the gnocchi into the boiling water. When they are floating aggressively, after 3 to 4 minutes of cooking, remove the gnocchi with a slotted spoon and transfer to the ice bath. Repeat with the remaining batches of gnocchi, and allow all the gnocchi to cool in the ice bath. Drain the cooked gnocchi well, stir in the olive oil, cover, and refrigerate until ready to cook. The gnocchi will keep in the fridge for up to 2 days.

When you are ready to serve the gnocchi, bring 6 quarts of water to a boil in a pasta pot and add 2 tablespoons of salt. Put the tomato sauce in a blender or a food processor and blend until smooth and homogeneous, then pour the sauce into a 12- to 14-inch sauté pan. Gently bring the sauce to a boil, then reduce the heat to maintain a simmer.

Continued on page 145.

Place the gnocchi into the pasta pot and cook until they all float, then use a slotted spoon or spider to carefully transfer the gnocchi to the pan with the sauce. Raise the heat to medium and toss gently for about 30 seconds. Tear the basil leaves into a few pieces, add to the pan, and toss together for 30 seconds more. Dump the pasta and sauce into a heated bowl and serve immediately.

BASIC TOMATO SAUCE

You need only 2 cups for this recipe, so save the rest for another day.

¼ cup extra-virgin olive oil

1 large Spanish onion, cut into
    ¼-inch dice

4 cloves garlic, thinly sliced

1 tablespoon chopped fresh thyme
    leaves, or 1 teaspoon dried

½ medium carrot, finely shredded

2 (28-ounce) cans whole San
    Marzano tomatoes, carefully
    crushed by hand, juices reserved

Kosher salt

In a 3-quart saucepan, heat the olive oil over medium heat. Add the onion and garlic and cook until soft and light golden brown, 8 to 10 minutes. Add the thyme and carrot and cook for 5 minutes more, until the carrot is quite soft. Add the tomatoes and their juices and bring to a boil, stirring often.

Reduce the heat to maintain a simmer and cook for 30 minutes, until as thick as hot cereal. Season with salt. This sauce will keep in an airtight container in the refrigerator for up to 1 week, or in the freezer for up to 6 months.

MAKES 4 CUPS

LINGUINE
with Kale Pesto

This easy pesto has a base component that will drive you crazy (as in happy) and lead you to a better and intuitive understanding of simple pastas and cooked and raw vegetables. The sky is truly the limit on variations!

SERVES 4 TO 6

2 cloves garlic

3 cups lightly packed kale leaves, stems and ribs removed, leaves roughly chopped

¼ cup sliced blanched almonds

Generous pinch of Maldon or other flaky sea salt

½ cup plus 2 tablespoons extra-virgin olive oil

½ cup freshly grated Pecorino Romano

2 tablespoons kosher salt

1 (1-pound) package linguine

Place the garlic in a food processor and pulse to chop it. Add the kale and pulse until finely chopped. Add the almonds and sea salt and, with the motor running, quickly drizzle in ½ cup of the oil. Transfer the pesto to a small bowl and stir in ¼ cup of the Pecorino Romano. (The pesto can be stored in a tightly sealed jar, topped with a thin layer of extra-virgin olive oil, in the refrigerator for 2 weeks.)

Bring 8 quarts of water to a boil in a large pot, and add the kosher salt. Place 1 cup of the pesto in a large, warmed serving bowl.

Cook the pasta according to the package instructions until just al dente. Just before draining, remove ½ cup of the pasta cooking water and place it in the bowl with the pesto.

Drain the pasta well and add it to the bowl with the pesto and pasta water. Toss the pasta to dress well.

Drizzle with the remaining 2 tablespoons oil and serve immediately with the remaining cheese on the side for sprinkling.

BAKED LASAGNE ALLA NORMA,

Sicilian Farmer–Style

I have never eaten this dish in Italia, but I imagine that a smart eggplant farmer must have. This is a case of intuition making sense; of course sweet eggplant works in the sauce with the béchamel and the tomato sauce…of course it does.

SERVES 8

FOR THE EGGPLANT-TOMATO SAUCE

3 tablespoons extra-virgin olive oil, plus more for the pan

2 medium eggplant, peeled and cut into medium dice

1 medium red onion, cut into ¼-inch dice

2 cloves garlic, thinly sliced

2 (28-ounce) cans Italian plum tomatoes, crushed by hand, juices reserved

3 tablespoons chopped fresh basil (about 2 large sprigs)

1 tablespoon fresh thyme leaves

Kosher salt and freshly ground black pepper

FOR THE BÉCHAMEL

5 tablespoons unsalted butter

¼ cup all-purpose flour

3 cups whole milk

2 teaspoons kosher salt

½ teaspoon freshly grated nutmeg

TO ASSEMBLE

2 tablespoons kosher salt

1 (1-pound) package lasagne pasta

1 cup freshly grated Parmigiano-Reggiano

MAKE THE EGGPLANT-TOMATO SAUCE

Preheat the oven to 475°F. Lightly oil a baking sheet.

Place the eggplant on the prepared baking sheet and roast until soft and dark golden brown, 15 to 20 minutes. Remove and allow to cool. Reduce the oven temperature to 375°F.

While the eggplant is roasting, heat the 3 tablespoons of olive oil in a 12- to 14-inch sauté pan until smoking. Add the onion and garlic and cook until soft and light golden brown, 5 to 6 minutes. Add the tomatoes, basil, and thyme and bring to a boil. Simmer for 15 minutes, and season with salt and pepper. Add the cooked eggplant cubes and simmer for about 6 minutes. Remove from the heat and set aside.

MAKE THE BÉCHAMEL

In a medium saucepan, melt the butter over medium heat. Add the flour and stir until smooth. Cook until light golden brown, about 5 minutes. Add the milk, 1 cup at a time, whisking continuously until smooth. Bring to a boil and cook for 5 minutes, season with the salt and nutmeg, and set aside.

ASSEMBLE THE DISH

Bring 8 quarts of water to a boil in a pasta pot and add the salt. Set up an ice bath next to the stovetop. Drop the pasta into the boiling water, 6 or 7 pieces at a time, and cook about 1 minute less than suggested on the package. Transfer to the ice bath to cool, then drain on kitchen towels, laying the pasta flat. Repeat to cook the rest of the pasta.

Spread a layer of the eggplant-tomato sauce over the bottom of a 9-by-13-inch lasagne pan and top with a sprinkling of Parmigiano, a layer of pasta, a layer of béchamel, another layer of eggplant-tomato sauce, a sprinkling of Parmigiano, and a layer of pasta. Repeat until all the ingredients are used up, finishing with a layer of pasta topped with béchamel and a sprinkling of Parmigiano.

Bake for 45 minutes, or until the edges are browned and the sauces are bubbling. Let stand for 10 minutes before serving.

Chicago

Chef:
PAUL KAHAN, THE PUBLICAN

Farmer:
DAVID CLEVERDON, KINNIKINNICK FARM

Ingredient:
ITALIAN BRAISING GREENS

Chef Paul Kahan was inspired by a salad. It wasn't a complicated salad. Its base was a head of baby escarole, and it was dressed with a creamy anchovy sauce.

He didn't want to replicate it for one of his Chicago restaurants. There was just something about it he really liked.

It was the baby escarole.

There was something exceedingly fresh about a salad built on the bitter green, and something unique and luxurious about the presentation of a whole head of it as an individual serving.

Luckily, Paul knows a guy.

He told David Cleverdon of Kinnikinnick Farm in northern Illinois about the salad and asked him if he could grow that kind of escarole for Paul's restaurants.

Let me look into it, David told him.

For David, farming wasn't so much a destination as the culmination of a lot of detours.

He came to Chicago in the 1960s to go to the University of Chicago, then got caught up in the civil rights movement. He says he worked for every good-intentioned, losing cause in the early 1960s.

He worked in politics on the Illinois governor's staff. The governor lost his bid for a second term, and David's time in politics was over. Then he worked at the Chicago Board of Trade, a commodities exchange that David calls a landing spot for misfits.

As a form of recreational labor, he gardened. Each season, he grew a little more, until he was pushing the capacity of his space. The bigger the garden got, the more he liked gardening. Eventually it became obvious that he didn't need a bigger garden. He needed a farm.

In the late 1980s, he and his wife, Susan, bought land about two hours north of Chicago. For more than two years, they came up from the city on weekends and worked to clean up the abandoned farmstead. It took months before they could run the mower without blowing out a tire. By the fourth year, they brought in a trailer to live in while the farmhouse was being restored, and David officially became a farmer.

He started off growing vegetables. He did it with purpose: He wanted to grow things to take to farmers' markets. He liked eating at some of the city's finest restaurants and wanted to grow food for them.

His first year at a farmers' market, he sold $47 worth of tomatoes.

Soon, he moved to the market at Evanston, the premier market in Chicago at the time. Chefs shop there, and they found his stand. David found himself making deals with chefs to grow things exclusively for them.

Paul likes David's braising greens, especially ones with an Italian accent.

Cavolo nero, otherwise known as Tuscan kale. Bietina, which is a sweet chard with a slight stem. Spigariello, a leafy broccoli. Minestra nera.

Wait. *Minestra nera* means "black soup." What is that?

One year, David stumbled upon a different variety of spigariello. He grew it, and he liked the flavor and texture of the heartier, curlier leaf. The packet included a long botanical name, but the words *minestra nera* were on there, too, so David called it that.

The challenge began the next season, when he bought the seed again but got a different plant. It was similar, but the leaves weren't curly and it didn't have the same flavor.

He bought more seeds and tried again. Same results.

He tracked down the original seed company in Italy and found a distributor. The distributor couldn't send it to the United States, so David needed to know a guy with the right license.

Of course David knows a guy.

He finally got the seeds…and got the wrong plant. Again.

He gave up on buying new seeds, but later found some of the original seeds in his barn. He planted them and finally got the plant he wanted. He planted the rest of his seeds in an undisclosed location in Michigan and plans to let them go to seed.

It's a long way to go for a braising green, but where else are you going to get minestra nera?

As David is making a delivery to The Publican, Paul's restaurant in a warehouse district west of the Loop in Chicago, he says we're about to learn something about lettuce.

The Little Gem Salad has always been on the menu at the restaurant. It is lettuce topped with fennel, radish, buttermilk vinaigrette, and pig's ears. It is always available, but that doesn't

mean Brian Huston, the restaurant's chef de cuisine, doesn't look for ways to improve it. Right now, he's looking at the lettuce.

Brian shows David how he constructs the salad with baby romaine. The long, narrow leaves lend themselves to stacking. That's not really how he wants to present the salad.

What he would like is a small head of butterhead lettuce, one that has uniform leaves that he can arrange like petals of a flower, "blooming" to hold the other elements.

Brian has one question: Is that possible?

David has several: Do you want each salad to come from a single head? How big should the largest leaves be? Do you want all the lettuce to be green, or a mix of green and red? How many heads do you need each week?

The chef answers all of the

farmer's questions. The farmer's answer to the chef's question was never in doubt.

By the end of the day, David has identified a variety of lettuce that grows to exactly the specifications Brian wants. Within a few weeks, he begins delivering them. By next season, a field will be dedicated to The Publican's Little Gem lettuce.

Turns out the baby escarole was possible, too.

David never found a variety of escarole that produced small heads, and because of the way escarole develops, it isn't as easy as just picking it young.

But David found that he could harvest a head just as it reaches its prime, then strip away a couple of outer leaves. It amounts to a heart of escarole. It's small. It's baby escarole.

He brings a few heads to show Paul. It's exactly what he wants.

It pays to know a guy.

Potato-Crusted
EGGPLANT AND ANGEL HAIR TURRETS

SERVES 4

4 tablespoons extra-virgin olive oil, plus more for drizzling

3 large eggs, lightly beaten

1 cup instant mashed potatoes (flakes)

1 eggplant, cut into ¼-inch-thick rounds

½ yellow onion, diced

2 cloves garlic, sliced

2 oil-packed anchovy fillets, plus 1 tablespoon of their packing oil

1 (28-ounce) can San Marzano tomatoes, crushed by hand, with their juices

1 teaspoon red pepper flakes

Kosher salt

1 (1-pound) package angel hair pasta

½ cup mozzarella, cut into small cubes

Fresh basil leaves, torn

¼ cup red pepper jelly

I made up this dish on the fly on The Chew and was surprised by how much we all loved it. I am a big fan of using instant mashed potato flakes for just about anything except mashed potatoes, so this gives me great joy!

In a large sauté pan, heat 2 tablespoons of the olive oil over medium-high heat. Line a plate with paper towels.

Place the eggs in a shallow dish, and the instant mashed potato flakes in a second shallow dish.

Dip the eggplant slices into the eggs, letting any excess drip off, and then dredge them in the instant potatoes, shaking off any excess. Fry the eggplant for 2 to 3 minutes per side, or until golden brown. Transfer to the paper towel–lined plate to drain.

In a large pot or small Dutch oven, heat the remaining 2 tablespoons olive oil over medium-high heat. Add the onion and sauté until slightly softened, 1 to 2 minutes. Add the garlic, anchovies, and tomatoes. Season with the red pepper flakes. Cook, uncovered, stirring occasionally, for 10 minutes, allowing the flavors to come together.

Bring a large pot of water to a rolling boil and season with salt. Cook the pasta for 1 minute less than instructed on the package. Drain the pasta, reserving 1 cup of the pasta cooking water.

Heat a large sauté pan over medium-high heat (you can wipe the pan clean that you used for the eggplant) and add a few ladlefuls of the pasta sauce. Add the pasta and cook for a minute; remove from the heat and add the mozzarella. Stir until the cheese is just melted and holding together.

Using an immersion blender, carefully puree the remaining tomato sauce in the pot.

Scoop a ladleful of the tomato sauce on a plate and spread to create a bed of sauce. Top with a slice of eggplant. Top with a twirl of pasta and some basil. Add another layer of eggplant, then pasta (a little less than the bottom layer) and basil, then top with an eggplant slice, a smear of pepper jelly, and some more fresh basil. Drizzle with olive oil and serve.

RIGATONI
with Lamb Ragu

Rich, fragrant slow-cooked lamb and pasta is a combination that whispers Rome and Sunday football in both Italiano and English. There may be no better dish for American sport worship.

SERVES 8 AS A FIRST COURSE, 4 AS A MAIN

¼ cup extra-virgin olive oil

1 onion, cut into ¼-inch dice

1 carrot, finely chopped

4 ounces pancetta, finely diced

1 bunch fresh mint, leaves only, finely chopped, plus 24 whole leaves

1 pound boneless lamb shoulder, cut into ¼-inch chunks

Kosher salt

Freshly ground black pepper

¼ cup tomato paste

1 cup dry red wine

2 cups Basic Tomato Sauce (page 145)

1 (1-pound) package rigatoni (I like DeCecco)

1 (1-pound) piece Pecorino Toscano (you will likely grate only ¼ pound of the cheese, but the large chunk will help you hold it as you grate)

In a deep, 10- to 12-inch sauté pan, heat the olive oil over medium-high heat until smoking. Add the onion, carrot, pancetta, and the chopped mint and cook until the pancetta has rendered its fat.

Season the lamb with salt and pepper, add it to the pan, and cook, stirring occasionally, until browned on all sides.

Add the tomato paste and cook until rust-colored, about 4 minutes, then add the wine and simmer for 5 minutes. Add the tomato sauce and bring to a boil, then reduce the heat to maintain a simmer, cover, and cook slowly for an hour, or until the meat is tender.

Bring 8 quarts of water to boil in a large pot, and add 2 tablespoons of salt.

Drop the pasta into the boiling water and cook for 2 minutes less than directed on the package. Drain the pasta, toss it into the pan with the sauce, add the whole mint leaves, and toss gently over medium-high heat for 1 minute.

Divide the pasta and sauce evenly among four warmed pasta bowls, and serve with the cheese on the side to grate over.

SPAGHETTI

with Fava Beans, Mint, and Garlic

Simple pastas using seasonal vegetables like favas are the warhorse of good value meets good nutrition on Happy Family Street. This is a prime example of such a culinary trifecta.

SERVES 4 TO 6

2 pounds young fava beans in the pod, shelled

Kosher salt

¼ cup extra-virgin olive oil

6 cloves garlic, thinly sliced

1 teaspoon red pepper flakes

1 (1-pound) package spaghetti

1 bunch fresh mint, leaves only, roughly chopped or torn

1 (1½-pound) chunk young Pecorino cheese, such as Pecorino Toscano (you will likely grate only ¼ pound of the cheese, but the large chunk will help you hold it as you grate)

If the fava beans are young and tender, there is no need to peel them. If not, blanch them in boiling water, then pinch open the skin at one end of each bean and squeeze out the bean, discarding the skin. Place the beans in a large bowl.

Bring 8 quarts of water to a boil in a pasta pot and add 2 tablespoons of salt.

In a 12-inch sauté pan, heat the oil, garlic, and red pepper flakes over medium heat until the garlic is light golden brown, about 2 minutes. Add the favas and cook until soft and lightly brown at the edges, about 2 minutes. Remove the pan from the heat and set aside.

Drop the spaghetti into the boiling water and cook for 1 minute less than directed on the package. Just before it is done, carefully ladle ¼ cup of the pasta cooking water into the pan with the favas. Drain the pasta in a colander and add to the pan with the fava mixture. Add the mint and place the pan over medium-high heat. Cook and toss to mix for 45 seconds until perfectly dressed.

Serve immediately in a warm dish, with the cheese on the side to grate over each portion.

RISI BISI

(Sweet Pea Risotto)

SERVES 4 TO 6

¼ cup extra-virgin olive oil

4 shallots, finely chopped

2 ribs celery, finely chopped

2 ounces prosciutto di San Daniele, cut into ⅛-inch dice

1½ cups arborio rice

8 cups chicken stock, heated

Kosher salt

2 pounds fresh peas, shelled to yield about 8 ounces, or 8 ounces frozen peas

4 tablespoons (½ stick) unsalted butter

½ cup freshly grated Parmigiano-Reggiano

Freshly ground black pepper

Risotto is served year-round near Venice and in Friuli, where there are more rice and corn fields than there are wheat fields. Each season has its own real superstar, and in Venice during pea season, this is the hero. The Venetians like their risotto all'onda, *which translates to "on the wave," meaning wet, not tight or dry, so do not cook it dry, but instead add an extra ladle of broth just before serving to keep it loosey-goosey.*

In a 10- to 12-inch sauté pan, heat the olive oil over medium heat. Add the shallots, celery, and prosciutto and cook until the shallots and celery are softened but not browned, 8 to 10 minutes.

Add the rice and stir for 2 minutes, until it is almost opaque. Add enough stock just to cover the rice, raise the heat to high, and bring to a boil. Cook, stirring, until the stock begins to be absorbed, then add another ladleful. As the level of stock dips below the level of the rice, continue to add stock, one ladleful at a time, to keep the rice covered, stirring continuously. After 15 minutes, taste the rice; it should still be quite hard. Season with salt at this point.

Add the peas and continue to cook for about 4 minutes more, adding a little more stock if necessary, until the rice is tender and creamy yet still al dente. The risotto should be quite moist, but not swimming (even so, you may have a little stock left over).

Remove from the heat, add the butter and Parmigiano, and stir vigorously for 25 seconds. Season with salt and pepper, divide the risotto among four warmed plates, and serve immediately.

Six:
MAIN DISHES

ALMOND-CRUSTED GROUPER "PICCATA"

One of my all-time favorite things to eat is a fried grouper sandwich with a cornflake crust, and this is a variation that celebrates crunchy crust and the creamy rich flavor of perhaps the most royal denizen of the Gulf of Mexico.

SERVES 4

¼ cup extra-virgin olive oil

½ cup finely chopped blanched almonds

Zest of 1 lemon

1 cup all-purpose flour

1 teaspoon kosher salt, plus more as needed

2 large eggs

4 (4- to 5-ounce) grouper fillets (or substitute whatever looks best at the market)

Freshly ground black pepper

½ cup dry white wine

3 tablespoons tiny capers

3 tablespoons unsalted butter, cold

Juice of 1 lemon

1 bunch fresh flat-leaf parsley, finely chopped (¼ cup)

Preheat the oven to 250°F.

In a large skillet, heat the oil over medium-high heat until just smoking.

In a shallow bowl, mix together the almonds, lemon zest, ½ cup of the flour, and the salt. In another shallow bowl, lightly beat the eggs. Place the remaining ½ cup flour in a third shallow bowl.

Season the fish with salt and pepper. Dredge each fish fillet in the unseasoned flour, then dip into the eggs, letting any excess drip off, and finally dredge in the almond mixture, patting gently to coat. Place the fish in the pan and cook for 3 to 4 minutes per side, until medium golden brown and nicely toasted, then transfer the fish to an ovenproof platter and place in the oven to keep warm.

Pour the oil out of the pan and wipe it quickly with a paper towel, then place it back on the burner. Add the wine and capers and bring to a boil. Cook for 30 seconds, then add the butter and lemon juice and swirl to make a sauce. Add the parsley, season with salt, and pour the sauce into little ramekins for dipping. Or pour the sauce over each serving of the warm fish.

SHRIMP STEW FROM PUGLIA

Sweet peppers combine perfectly with delicious sweet and briny shrimp in this dish. Try to find American Gulf shrimp—they are truly the best in the world, and by serving them we support our local fisheries.

SERVES 4

6 tablespoons extra-virgin olive oil, plus more for drizzling

1 red onion, cut into ⅛-inch dice

2 red bell peppers, seeded and cut into ⅛-inch dice

2 yellow bell peppers, seeded and cut into ⅛-inch dice

1 teaspoon red pepper flakes

1 tablespoon sugar

½ cup Basic Tomato Sauce (page 145)

Kosher salt and freshly ground black pepper

2 pounds (16/20-count) shrimp, peeled and deveined, shells reserved for stock

3 cups Shrimp Stock (recipe below)

½ bunch fresh chives, cut into 3-inch lengths

In a 10- to 12-inch sauté pan, heat 2 tablespoons of the olive oil over high heat until just smoking. Add the onion and bell peppers and sauté for 5 minutes. Add the red pepper flakes, sugar, tomato sauce, and salt and black pepper to taste and cook over low heat until tender, about 10 minutes. Remove from the heat and set aside.

In a 12- to 14-inch sauté pan, heat the remaining 4 tablespoons olive oil over high heat until smoking. Season the shrimp with salt and black pepper on both sides and cook until very red, 1 to 2 minutes. Turn carefully with a wide spatula and cook on the other side for 1 minute. You may need to cook the shrimp in batches to avoid overcrowding the pan.

Remove the shrimp, add the bell pepper mixture and the shrimp stock to the pan, and bring to a boil. Cook for 3 minutes, then return the shrimp to the mix and reduce the heat to maintain a simmer for a few minutes more.

Ladle the stew into deep bowls and garnish with chives and a drizzle of good olive oil.

SHRIMP STOCK

1 tablespoon olive oil

Reserved shells from 2 pounds shrimp

2 tablespoons sweet paprika or sweet pimentón

4 cups water

Kosher salt

In a 3- to 4-quart saucepan, heat the olive oil over medium heat.

Add the shrimp shells and toss well. Allow the shells to cook for 2 to 3 minutes, stirring often. Add the sweet paprika and cook for 3 minutes more.

Add the water and bring to a simmer, pressing down on the shells with a spatula or large spoon to extract maximum flavor. Cook until reduced by one-quarter, then turn off the heat.

Pour the stock through a fine-mesh strainer into a saucepan, pressing down on the shells until all the liquid is extracted; discard the shells.

Season with a little salt to taste.

GRILLED SALMON

with Strawberry Salsa

SERVES 4

1½ pints fresh strawberries (3 cups), hulled and rinsed

4 cloves garlic, minced

4 jalapeños, 2 seeded and minced, 2 roasted, skinned, and chopped

½ red onion, cut into ⅛-inch dice

1 chipotle chile in adobo (available at Latin specialty stores), chopped into a paste

1 tablespoon extra-virgin olive oil, plus more for drizzling

Zest and juice of 1 lime

4 scallions, thinly sliced

2 tablespoons chopped fresh cilantro

1 teaspoon honey

4 (5- to 6-ounce) salmon fillets

Kosher salt and freshly ground black pepper

I grew up on the West Coast, and grilling salmon was a huge part of the late-summer weekend experience along with listening to baseball on the radio in the backyard while we did our chores. Local strawberries always added sweet and tangy deliciousness to every single meal when they were in season, and salmon was no exception.

Chop the strawberries into ¼-inch pieces and toss them in a bowl with the garlic, jalapeños, red onion, chipotle paste, oil, lime zest, lime juice, scallions, cilantro, and honey and stir to mix.

Preheat the grill or broiler. Season each salmon fillet with salt and pepper and grill until medium rare, 4 to 5 minutes on each side.

Season the salsa with salt while the salmon is cooking.

Place the salmon on a plate, spoon salsa over the top, drizzle with oil, and serve.

PERFECT ROASTED CHICKEN

There is almost nothing more satisfying both to cook and to eat than roasted chicken, and this is my best recipe for Sunday supper. Michael Symon and I continue our debate on whether to brine or not to brine, and I must say that when we had a taste test, even he chose the brined bird. Brining is about salinity and timing, so if there is a question, always brine for less time, not more. For very crisp skin, it is always better to brine the day before and allow the bird to dry in the fridge overnight, uncovered.

SERVES 4

FOR THE BRINE

1 cup kosher salt

1 stick cinnamon

1 bunch fresh rosemary

½ cup apple cider

2 quarts boiling water

2 quarts ice

FOR THE CHICKEN

1 (2½- to 3-pound) free-range chicken

3 tablespoons extra-virgin olive oil

2 tablespoons kosher salt

2 tablespoons freshly ground black pepper

1 lemon, thinly sliced

1 bunch fresh thyme

8 cloves garlic

6 sprigs fresh marjoram

1 small red onion, thinly sliced

MAKE THE BRINE

In a plastic container or stainless-steel bowl large enough to hold the chicken, stir the salt, cinnamon, rosemary, and cider together. Pour in the boiling water and stir to dissolve. Add the ice and stir. Submerge the chicken in the brine. Place a plate on top of the bird to prevent it from floating. The chicken should be completely submerged throughout the brining process. Cover and refrigerate for 1 to 4 hours, but no longer. Pour off the brine, then dry the chicken thoroughly with paper towels. Place the brined bird on a plate and place in the refrigerator to air-dry, uncovered, for at least another hour, or—even better—overnight, before roasting.

MAKE THE CHICKEN

Preheat the oven to 475°F.

Remove the chicken from the refrigerator and let stand at room temperature for 30 minutes.

Rub the whole chicken with the olive oil. In a small bowl, mix the salt and pepper and season the chicken inside and out with the mixture. Place 1 slice of lemon under the skin of each breast, centered beautifully. Place the thyme, garlic, marjoram, remaining lemon slices, and onion in the chicken's cavity.

Continued on page 172.

Place the chicken on a rack set inside a roasting pan. Roast the chicken for 20 minutes, then reduce the temperature to 375°F. Continue cooking the chicken until the thigh juices run clear and an instant-read thermometer inserted into the thickest part of the thigh, away from the bone, registers 160°F, about 30 minutes more. Transfer the chicken to a warmed platter in a warm place and let rest for 10 to 15 minutes. Carve and serve.

CHICKEN AND DUMPLINGS

I have learned a lot about the true cooking of the South from Carla Hall at The Chew, *and this is my take on her version of Chicken and Dumplings. I like the earthy flavor of the whole wheat flour in the drop biscuit topping, and it makes Dafo happy, too.*

SERVES 8

FOR THE CHICKEN

1 (6-pound) organic roaster chicken

Coarse salt and freshly ground black pepper

3 tablespoons unsalted butter

2 tablespoons extra-virgin olive oil

3 tablespoons all-purpose flour

2 ribs celery, cut into ¼-inch pieces

2 large carrots, cut into ¼-inch rounds

2 leeks, cut into ¼-inch rounds, rinsed and drained

4 slices Homemade Bacon (recipe follows) or store-bought, thinly sliced into batonettes

2 sprigs fresh thyme

3 cups chicken stock

1 cup dry white wine

FOR THE DUMPLINGS

1 cup whole wheat flour

1 tablespoon baking powder

Leaves from 2 bunches fresh tarragon, chopped

½ cup plus 1 tablespoon half-and-half

1 teaspoon kosher salt

Freshly ground black pepper

MAKE THE CHICKEN

Preheat the oven to 400°F.

Cut the chicken into 10 serving pieces and discard the back.

Aggressively season the chicken pieces with coarse salt and pepper. Heat the butter and olive oil in a braising pot over medium-high heat. Brown the chicken pieces, working in batches if necessary, for 7 to 8 minutes per side. Transfer to a plate, leaving the fat in the pot. Add the flour and stir to make a roux, mix well, and cook for 1 minute. Reduce the heat to medium-low, add the vegetables, bacon, and thyme and cook for 15 minutes. Add the stock and the wine, bring to a boil, and season with salt and pepper. Return the chicken to the pot, cover, and bake for 30 minutes.

MAKE THE DUMPLINGS

Meanwhile, in a bowl, combine the whole wheat flour, baking powder, half of the tarragon, the half-and-half, and kosher salt.

Take the pot with the chicken out of the oven (leaving the oven on), remove the lid, and scoop 1-tablespoon dollops of the dumpling mixture on top of the chicken mixture—you should end up with about 10 dumplings. Cover the pot and return to the oven for 10 minutes. Remove from the oven, sprinkle with the remaining tarragon and a bit of ground black pepper, and serve immediately.

Continued on page 175.

HOMEMADE BACON

MAKES 2 POUNDS

1 teaspoon pink salt (also called Prague Powder No. 1)

2 tablespoons kosher salt

¼ cup freshly ground black pepper

1 teaspoon freshly grated nutmeg

¼ cup pure, grade A maple syrup

6 cloves garlic, smashed

3 tablespoons crushed juniper berries

10 sprigs fresh thyme, roughly chopped

1 (2-pound) piece raw, uncured pork belly, skin removed (ask your butcher for the thickest piece available)

Making bacon at home takes a little time, but once you try your own, you will use commercial bacon only when you're in a pinch. You can change the spice profile any way you would like—just keep the pink salt and kosher salt ratios in order with the weight of the raw belly.

In a bowl, stir together the pink salt, kosher salt, pepper, nutmeg, maple syrup, garlic, juniper, and thyme and mix well to make a paste. Place the pork belly on a cutting board and massage all over with the paste, making sure that the paste covers the entire surface of the pork belly. Place in a zip-top bag, seal, and refrigerate for 7 days.

Preheat your smoker or grill to 225°F.

Remove the pork belly from the bag, rinse off the curing paste, and pat dry. Place the pork belly in the smoker or grill and cook until it registers 155°F on a meat thermometer, 90 to 120 minutes, then remove and let cool. Your bacon is ready to eat. You can slice it and fry it like store-bought bacon, happy in the knowledge that yours is better. Wrap it tightly in plastic wrap and store in the fridge for up to 3 months.

CHICKEN SALTIMBOCCA

I use boneless, skinless thighs as the base of this recipe, and the prosciutto yields a fine, durable, crisp crust to the final dish. Be sure to cook it until it becomes a nice deep golden brown with an almost leathery texture, which softens slightly in the sweet marsala bath.

SERVES 4

1 cup all-purpose flour

Kosher salt and freshly ground black pepper

8 boneless, skinless chicken thighs

8 large fresh sage leaves

8 large slices prosciutto

¼ cup extra-virgin olive oil

4 shallots, thinly sliced

1 pound of a mix of cremini and oyster mushrooms, cut into ¼-inch pieces

1 cup sweet marsala wine

½ cup chicken stock

2 tablespoons unsalted butter

1 bunch fresh flat-leaf parsley, finely chopped (¼ cup)

Place the flour in a shallow bowl and season with salt and pepper. Lightly pound the chicken thighs to ¼-inch thickness. Season with salt and pepper and lay a sage leaf on each thigh. Lay 1 slice prosciutto over each thigh and fold in half like a book. Secure the two sides with a toothpick and dredge the whole piece in the seasoned flour.

In a 12- to 14-inch sauté pan, heat the oil until just smoking. Add the chicken and sauté until golden brown on both sides, then transfer to a plate. Add the shallots and mushrooms to the pan and cook until the mushrooms have sweated out their liquid, 5 to 6 minutes. Add the marsala and chicken stock and cook over high heat until reduced by half. Return the chicken thighs to the pan with the sauce and simmer for 3 minutes. Swirl in the butter, add the parsley, and serve.

Tampa

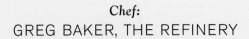

Chef:
GREG BAKER, THE REFINERY

Farmer:
REBECCA KRASSNOSKI,
NATURE DELIVERED FARM

Ingredient:
PORK

Chef Greg Baker was planning his dish for a fund-raiser. The menu was to be a celebration of foods from Florida, and he decided to make Mojo Pork Belly with White Beans and Chorizo.

Citrus often gets billing as the state's synonymous foodstuff, but it's possible that nothing is more Floridian than pork. Legend has it that Hernando de Soto landed near Tampa Bay in 1539 with thirteen pigs in tow, and that America's pork industry can trace its roots back to that herd.

Bacon practically started here.

For his restaurant, The Refinery, Greg takes pains to buy ingredients from farms that raise animals humanely and sustainably. For a long time, that meant his pork was coming from as far away as Tennessee.

For this dish, he needed pork that had been raised much closer to home.

A mutual friend introduced Greg to Rebecca Krassnoski, who was raising pigs on a small farm in Hernando County, which is, coincidentally or not, named after our pork-loving conquistador.

Rebecca loaded up the bellies and drove south on Interstate 75 while Greg headed north. They met in a chain restaurant's parking lot, exchanged pleasantries and pork, then turned around and went back to work.

Unconventional deliveries are nothing new for Rebecca.

When she delivers her pigs for processing, she makes an impression. A form the processor fills out when live animals are accepted includes a line that asks how the animals were unloaded from the trailer.

Answers might include a paddle, which annoys pigs out of the trailer. Or a board, which forces them out. Or an electric prod, which does exactly what it sounds like.

Those are the allowable methods. There are stories about what happens when no one is watching.

There are also stories about how Rebecca unloads her pigs.

"Blueberry doughnut!" the man radios in to officials filling out the form.

The pigs often walk out to their fate just because Rebecca tells them to. But if they don't, she has a couple of pastries on hand. A blueberry doughnut almost always works, and if it doesn't, Rebecca takes the pig back home.

The lack of drama is testament to how the pigs spend their seven-month lives on Rebecca's farm. There are no barns. No concrete stalls. Certainly no gestation crates. There are a few electric fences—more to keep other animals out than hers in—and an almost comical array of roofing pallets arranged in such a way as to imply pens. But her pigs are contained mostly by their own complicity.

There is pig farming in Rebecca's family tree. Her grandfather raised them on a farm in a Western Pennsylvania valley in the 1960s, on land ceded to the family as thanks for fighting in the Revolutionary War. But it wasn't a genetic calling that got her into the business.

It was the economy.

She worked as an estimator for a construction company. That was a good job in Florida, until suddenly it wasn't anymore. She started thinking about ways to call her own shots.

Farming was a dream. She was drawn to the idea of raising pigs because she thought they were the most mistreated animals in the food chain, and they were among the smartest, making it worse.

There is no book on how to establish a niche, farrow-to-finish, pastured pig farm in rural Florida. She sought mentors and studied her grandfather's herd log from the 1960s, guidelines of a certification program, any book she could find. But for the most part, she would be farming by karma. Do good things and hope it comes back.

She wanted feed that wasn't genetically modified, but that's expensive. A friend of a friend was making craft beer and had spent grain, food for the price of the gas it took to pick it up. At a farmers' market, she saw a vendor carving fresh pineapple, producing hundreds of pounds of scrap. Rebecca saw pig treats. The vendor was happy to have them hauled off. It didn't eliminate her food bill, but helped mitigate it. And it made the pigs happy.

But karma can backfire.

One day, several bellies after they met, Greg told her his plan for a new project, one that would require more pork. Hypothetically, he asked, could she provide him more pigs per month?

For Rebecca, this wasn't just an increase in business; she was being included in the creative process.

She could ramp up production for a new venture, she told him. Just say the word.

Then she thought, *Why wait?* If she started now, she could work out kinks before anyone was counting on the pigs. She hoped her initiative would impress Greg. What could go wrong?

It became apparent almost immediately.

More pigs eat more food. More food costs more money. But until the pigs are sold, there isn't more money.

Rebecca was in trouble. She started considering options. She could take the pigs to auction, tantamount to a total personal failure. She'd get pennies to send her pigs into her nightmare. She told Greg the story: She needed to sell fifteen pigs immediately or she would go out of business.

Give me an hour, Greg said.

Greg and a friend who works as an intermediary between farmers and restaurants tapped a fraternity of chefs, making appeals to their sense of community. Greg bought two pigs. Another restaurant wanted two. So did another. One wanted one. A caterer wanted one. So did another. The next day, a chef at a hotel bought three. Another heard and matched the order. That was fifteen.

Disaster was averted. Rebecca calls it her "bailout."

Or maybe it was a stimulus package.

Rebecca has since moved her pigs to a ninety-acre farmstead where they will work in concert with other farmers' goats, cows, and chickens. Her pigs will live on different plots on the farm, taking turns with the other animals. Each herd takes something different from the spot and makes its own contribution to the soil to prepare it for the crops that will ultimately grow there. When humans orchestrate this process, it's called multispecies rotational grazing, or permaculture. When humans don't orchestrate it, it's called nature.

It may not be as cool as a patch of rolling hills handed to your ancestors by the founding fathers, but it'll do.

BBQ CHICKEN THIGHS

with Lentils and Green Apple Vinaigrette

You can easily cook these in the oven and still get spectacular texture and flavor. Simply put them on a greased baking sheet, skin side up, and cook them at 450°F until they're almost charred.

SERVES 6 TO 8

12 cloves garlic, 10 crushed, 2 finely chopped

½ cup plus 3 tablespoons extra-virgin olive oil, plus more as needed

2 salt-packed anchovies, filleted, rinsed, and patted dry

1 bunch fresh flat-leaf parsley, finely chopped (¼ cup)

2 cups fresh bread crumbs

12 boneless, skin-on chicken thighs

Kosher salt

2 shallots, finely chopped

1 cup dried lentils, rinsed and picked over

2 cups water

1 carrot, cut into ⅛-inch dice

2 scallions, thinly sliced

2 tablespoons red wine vinegar

12 tablespoons Green Apple Vinaigrette (recipe below)

Combine the 10 cloves of crushed garlic, ½ cup of olive oil, the anchovies, parsley, and bread crumbs in a food processor and process until smooth.

Season the chicken thighs with salt and a drizzle of oil. Put the chicken thighs in a large bowl and sprinkle with the bread-crumb mixture, turning to coat well. Arrange them in a single layer on a platter, cover, and refrigerate for at least 15 minutes, or up to overnight.

Prepare a gas or charcoal grill for indirect grilling, or preheat the oven to 450°F.

Oil the grill grates well. Place the chicken thighs, skin side up, on the cooler part of the grill, close the grill top, and grill until the chicken is cooked through, turning once, about 15 minutes per side.

Meanwhile, heat the 3 tablespoons of oil in a 10- to 12-inch sauté pan over medium heat. Add the remaining 2 cloves of chopped garlic and the shallots, and cook, stirring occasionally, until the shallots are soft, about 5 minutes. Add the lentils and water, bring to a boil, and cook, stirring, just until tender, about 30 minutes. Remove from the heat, add the carrot, scallions, and vinegar, and stir to combine. Transfer the lentils to a platter and set aside.

Arrange the grilled chicken pieces on top of the lentils and serve with a tablespoon of the vinaigrette over each thigh.

GREEN APPLE VINAIGRETTE

1 Granny Smith apple

¼ cup red wine vinegar

1 tablespoon Dijon mustard

½ cup extra-virgin olive oil

Peel and core the apple and cut it into ⅛-inch dice. Place the apple pieces in a medium bowl and add the vinegar, mustard, and olive oil. Stir to combine. The dressing should not emulsify but rather remain wet and broken with rivulets of oil.

MAKES 1 CUP

CHICKEN A LA CACCIATORA

"Hunter's-style" chicken may or may not involve whatever your hunter brings home from the hunt, but it usually involves mushrooms and rosemary in my house, where most of the hunting is done at the Union Square Greenmarket or at Eataly.

SERVES 4

8 cloves garlic, chopped

Leaves from 1 sprig fresh rosemary, minced

2 tablespoons kosher salt, plus more as needed

2 tablespoons freshly ground black pepper, plus more as needed

½ cup extra-virgin olive oil

1 (3-pound) organic broiler chicken, cut into 8 serving pieces

1 ounce dried porcini mushrooms

1 cup very hot water

2 large red onions, cut into ½-inch dice

1 pound cremini mushrooms, halved

4 ounces pancetta, cut into 1-inch dice

2 bulbs fennel, cut into ½-inch dice, fronds chopped and reserved

2 carrots, cut into 1-inch pieces

1 (6-ounce) can tomato paste

1 cup dry white wine

1 cup chicken stock

Pinch of red pepper flakes

1 bunch fresh flat-leaf parsley, finely chopped (¼ cup)

In a large bowl, combine the garlic, rosemary, salt, and black pepper, and add enough of the olive oil (3 to 4 tablespoons) to make a somewhat dry paste. Add the chicken and rub the paste evenly over the pieces of chicken. Cover and refrigerate for at least 2 hours or up to overnight.

Place the dried porcini in a bowl and pour the water over them. Set aside to reconstitute for 15 minutes.

In a Dutch oven, heat the remaining ¼ cup olive oil over high heat until smoking. Brush the excess paste from the chicken pieces and sear, in batches if necessary, until browned on all sides. Transfer to a plate and keep warm.

Add the onions, cremini, pancetta, fennel, and carrots to the pot, · season with salt and black pepper, and cook until the onions are golden brown and the pancetta has rendered its fat, about 10 minutes. Drain off the excess oil, then add the tomato paste and cook for about 5 minutes over medium heat, until it is rust-colored. Add the wine and stir with a wooden spoon to dislodge the browned bits from the bottom of the pot. Add the stock, the porcini and their soaking liquid, and the red pepper flakes and bring to a boil.

Return the chicken to the pot, cover, reduce the heat to medium, and cook for 20 minutes. Uncover and cook until cooked through, 5 to 10 minutes more. Transfer the chicken to a festive platter, stir the fennel fronds and parsley into the vegetable mixture, top with the sauce, and serve.

CHICKEN FLAUTAS

with Pickled Jalapeño Pico de Gallo

MAKES 12 FLAUTAS

FOR THE FLAUTAS

2 pounds boneless, skinless chicken thighs

Kosher salt and freshly ground black pepper

¼ cup plus 3 tablespoons extra-virgin olive oil

2 Spanish onions, cut into ¼-inch dice

1 teaspoon ground cumin

3 cloves garlic, crushed

½ pound tomatillos, husks removed, washed well, and halved

1 cup water

3 jalapeños, chopped, seeds and all

½ bunch fresh cilantro, finely chopped

Zest and juice of 2 limes

1 bunch scallions, thinly sliced

12 (8-inch) flour tortillas

FOR THE PICO DE GALLO

4 ripe plum tomatoes, cut into ⅛-inch dice

4 pickled jalapeños, cut into ⅛-inch dice

2 serrano chiles, cut into ⅛-inch dice

Zest and juice of 1 lemon

½ bunch fresh cilantro, finely chopped

TO ASSEMBLE

Vegetable oil, for frying

Kosher salt and ground black pepper

We usually make these delicious crisp winners the day after roasted chicken night, using leftovers. But here is the recipe if you're starting from scratch. The success of the dish is dependent on the amount of love you put in with the chicken filling…Be bold, add more.

MAKE THE FLAUTAS

Season the chicken thighs all over with salt and pepper. In a large sauté pan, heat the ¼ cup of olive oil until smoking. Add the chicken and brown on both sides. Transfer to a plate. Add the remaining 3 tablespoons olive oil, the onions, cumin, garlic, tomatillos, and water to the pan and bring to a boil. Return the chicken pieces to the pan, return to a boil, reduce the heat to maintain a simmer, and cook for 20 minutes, until cooked through. Remove from the heat and allow to cool. Remove the chicken, shred it, and set aside. Puree the tomatillo mixture in a blender and pour it into a bowl. Add the shredded chicken to the sauce mixture and add the jalapeños, the cilantro, the lime zest, lime juice, and scallions and stir to mix well. Season with salt and allow the filling to cool.

Warm the tortillas in the microwave for 1 minute. Working with 1 warm tortilla at a time, spread 2 full tablespoons of the filling across the center of each tortilla. Roll up the tortilla and close each at the seam with a wooden toothpick. Cover the rolled tortillas with a moist towel. The flautas may be prepared to this point up to 4 hours in advance.

MAKE THE PICO DE GALLO

Place the tomatoes in a bowl with the pickled jalapeños and the serranos, then add the lemon zest, lemon juice, and cilantro and stir. Set aside.

ASSEMBLE THE DISH

In a large skillet, heat 1 inch of vegetable oil over moderately high heat until it registers 360°F on a deep-fry thermometer. Fry the flautas in batches, seam side down, turning them, for 1 to 2 minutes, or until they are crisp. As they are finished, use tongs to transfer them to paper towels to drain. Season with salt while still very hot.

Season the pico de gallo with salt and pepper. Serve the flautas with the pico de gallo.

JERK CHICKEN

with Spicy Pineapple Ketchup and Roti

SERVES 8

FOR THE MARINADE

1 medium red onion, finely chopped

1 bunch scallions, chopped

¼ cup Tabasco Chipotle Sauce

Zest and juice of 2 limes

Zest and juice of 2 lemons

Zest and juice of 1 orange

2 tablespoons molasses

2 tablespoons honey

1 tablespoon dried thyme

2 tablespoons ground allspice

1 teaspoon freshly grated nutmeg

2 teaspoons pure vanilla extract

1 teaspoon kosher salt

FOR THE CHICKEN

8 chicken thighs

Kosher salt and freshly ground black pepper

Spicy Pineapple Ketchup (recipe follows)

8 West Indies Roti (flatbread) (recipe follows)

On a hot summer evening there is nothing that cools me down better than this spicy Jamaican-inspired chicken. The pineapple ketchup cuts the heat with sweet, and the bread brings it all together, like Bunny Wailer still does.

MAKE THE MARINADE

In a large bowl, combine all the ingredients for the marinade.

MAKE THE CHICKEN

Put the chicken pieces in a tight-sealing plastic container and pour the marinade over. Toss well to coat everywhere. Refrigerate for at least 4 hours—overnight is best.

Preheat the oven to 450°F or light your grill with one side hot, one side low.

Remove the chicken from the marinade and discard the marinade. Season with salt and pepper. Place on a baking sheet and roast for 40 minutes; it should get a little char on the top (we like that). If using a grill, place the chicken on the hot side of the grill and cook until nicely charred on both sides, then move to the cooler side and cook with the lid down until cooked through.

Serve hot, with pineapple ketchup and warm roti alongside.

Continued on page 190.

SPICY PINEAPPLE KETCHUP

2 cups pineapple, cut into
⅟₂-inch pieces

1 medium red onion, cut into
⅛-inch dice

2 serrano chiles, stemmed

1 tablespoon honey

1 tablespoon Worcestershire sauce

¼ cup ketchup

½ cup pineapple juice

Zest and juice of 1 lime

2 cloves garlic, sliced

1 teaspoon kosher salt

Place all the ingredients in a food processor and pulse until smooth. If not using immediately, store in a sealed container in the refrigerator for up to 1 week.

MAKES 3 CUPS

WEST INDIES ROTI (FLATBREAD)

4 cups all-purpose flour

2 teaspoons baking powder

1 teaspoon kosher salt

¼ cup extra-virgin olive oil

1 cup water

Combine the dry ingredients in a stand mixer fitted with the dough hook. Turn the mixer on and gradually add the oil and water while mixing, then mix for 5 minutes. Remove the dough from the mixer and let rest for 10 minutes.

Divide the dough into 8 equal balls. Flatten each slightly and roll out into 6-inch rounds.

Heat a cast-iron skillet over high heat until a drop of water sizzles on the surface. Reduce the heat to medium and place the rotis in the pan, 2 at a time, and cook for 2 to 3 minutes, until the crust is light brown. Turn with a wide spatula and cook for 1 minute on the other side. Repeat with the remaining dough and keep warm in a bowl, covered with a clean dish towel.

MAKES 8 ROTI

CHICKEN POTPIES

with Chard and Peas

Comfort food for me is almost always pasta or a breakfast item, but these potpies truly bring comfort food to another level. The chard is unexpected and yet brings a smooth joy to the sauce and a real mineral bump that I love.

SERVES 8

FOR THE PIE FILLING

5 cups chicken stock, preferably homemade

8 boneless, skin-on chicken thighs

Kosher salt and freshly ground black pepper

8 tablespoons (1 stick) unsalted butter

2 Spanish onions, cut into ¼-inch dice

3 medium carrots, cut into ½-inch dice

1 bunch Swiss chard, finely chopped

½ cup all-purpose flour

½ cup whole milk

2 cups frozen peas

2 bunches fresh flat-leaf parsley, finely chopped (½ cup)

Leaves from 1 bunch fresh tarragon, finely chopped (3 tablespoons)

FOR THE PASTRY

3 cups all-purpose flour

2 teaspoons kosher salt

1 teaspoon baking powder

16 tablespoons (2 sticks) unsalted butter, cold, diced

½ cup ice water, or as needed

TO ASSEMBLE

1 egg beaten with 1 tablespoon water, for egg wash

Flaked sea salt

MAKE THE PIE FILLING

Place the chicken stock in a 6-quart saucepan and bring to a boil over medium-high heat. Season the chicken thighs with salt and pepper and drop them into the stock. Return to a boil and simmer for 6 minutes, or until cooked through. Remove the chicken thighs and let cool (keep the stock hot). Remove the skin and discard it (or fry it up for a little snack). Cut the chicken into 1-inch dice. You will have about 5 cups cubed chicken.

In a large pot or Dutch oven, melt the butter over medium-low heat. Add the onions, carrots, and chopped chard and sauté until the onions are translucent, 8 to 10 minutes. Add the flour, reduce the heat to low, and cook, stirring continuously, for 2 minutes. Add the hot chicken stock to the sauce. Simmer, stirring, for 10 minutes, or until thick. Add 1 tablespoon salt, 1 teaspoon pepper, and the milk. Add the cubed chicken, the peas, parsley, and tarragon. Mix well.

MAKE THE CRUST

Whisk together the flour, salt, and baking powder in a medium bowl. With a pastry blender or two knives, cut in the butter until the mixture resembles coarse crumbs. Drizzle 3 tablespoons of the ice water over the flour mixture, tossing with a fork to moisten it evenly, then add more water, about 1 teaspoon at a time, until the dough comes together (you may not need to use all the water). Gather the dough into a ball, wrap in plastic wrap, and chill for at least 30 minutes.

Continued on page 192.

Preheat the oven to 375°F.

Divide the chicken mixture evenly among 8 serving-size ovenproof bowls. Divide the dough into 8 balls and roll each piece into a circle at least an inch wider than the top of the bowls. Brush the outside edges of each bowl with the egg wash, then place the dough on top. Press the dough against the side of the bowls to make each piece stick. Brush the dough with egg wash and make an X-shaped vent in the top. Sprinkle with sea salt and place on a baking sheet. Bake for 1 hour, or until the top is golden brown and the filling is bubbling.

SPANISH CHICKEN

with Saffron, Onions, and Olives

SERVES 4

1 tablespoon kosher salt

2 teaspoons ground cayenne

1 (3- to 3½-pound) organic fryer chicken, cut into 10 serving pieces

3 tablespoons extra-virgin olive oil

1 tablespoon all-purpose flour

1 teaspoon saffron

8 cups julienne onions (about 2½ pounds)

½ cup Moroccan olives

1 cup chicken stock

1 bunch fresh cilantro, roughly chopped (optional)

Seeds from 1 pomegranate, for serving (optional)

2 scallions, thinly sliced (optional)

This was without a doubt my favorite dish in high school, and my mom nailed it every time. The fragrance of the saffron as it cooks is intoxicating, and the contrast in the flavor of the sweet onions and the briny, salty olives creates harmony that glows hot and bright from within.

In a small bowl, mix together the salt and cayenne and season the chicken pieces with the mixture. In a large cast-iron skillet, heat the oil until smoking. Brown the chicken pieces, cooking them for 6 to 8 minutes on each side. Transfer the chicken to a plate as it is cooked. Add the flour, saffron, and onions to the skillet. Add any remaining salt and cayenne mixture. Cook, stirring continuously, to wilt and brown the onions, scraping the bottom of the pan to loosen any browned particles, about 10 minutes. Add the chicken pieces and the olives. Continue stirring, again scraping the bottom of the pot to loosen any browned particles, and cook for about 15 minutes. Add the chicken stock, cover, and reduce the heat to medium. Cook, stirring occasionally, for about 15 minutes, or until the chicken is tender.

Place on a swanky platter and sprinkle with chopped cilantro, pomegranate seeds, and scallions, if using.

CHICKEN SCARPARIELLO

with Sweet and Hot Peppers

MAKES 6 SERVINGS

6 tablespoons extra-virgin olive oil

8 bone-in, skin-on chicken thighs

2 sweet Italian sausages, cut into 6 pieces each

1 pound new potatoes, scrubbed and quartered

1 medium red onion, cut into ½-inch dice

10 cloves garlic

4 red bell peppers, seeded and cut into ½-inch dice

6 whole small hot peppers, such as cayenne or serrano

1 cup dry white wine, plus more as needed

1 cup hot water

Leaves from 1 bunch fresh basil, chopped

1 bunch fresh flat-leaf parsley, finely chopped (¼ cup)

Scarpariello is "shoemaker" in Italian. Here, "shoemaker's" chicken may refer to Neapolitan shoemakers making delicious food in the little time they had at the end of the day, but I am pretty sure it is not a traditional dish in Italia. It is probably more a "Little Italy" dish, born of southern Italian roots somewhere in our great Italian American neighborhoods here in the United States. In any case, it is delicious, piquant, and very easy to make.

In a 10- to 12-inch heavy-bottomed sauté pan, heat the olive oil over high heat until smoking. Add the chicken pieces, skin side down, working in batches if necessary to avoid crowding the pan, and brown on both sides, turning once. Transfer to a plate and set aside. In the same pan, cook the sausage slices and potatoes until brown; remove them and set aside with the chicken. Drain off half of the fat from the pan.

Add the onion, garlic, bell peppers, and hot peppers to the pan and sauté until golden brown, about 10 minutes. Add the wine and water and bring to a boil. Return the chicken, sausage, and potatoes to the pan, reduce the heat to medium-low, and cook at a bubbling simmer until cooked through, 25 to 30 minutes; add more wine or water if necessary to keep the pan from getting dry.

Transfer the chicken to serving plates. Stir the basil and parsley into the sauce remaining in the pan and spoon over the chicken. Serve with 1 hot pepper atop each portion.

CHICKEN KIEV
with Goat Cheese and Chopped Greens

This is an adaptation of my dear mother-in-law Lillian Cahn's take on the Russian classic. She added the goat cheese and I added the tarragon and kale. It would have made her very happy to see this, may she rest in peace. She was a glorious spirit and radiates light to this day.

SERVES 6 TO 8

¼ cup extra-virgin olive oil

2 cloves garlic, thinly sliced

1 bunch (½ pound) lacinato kale, cut into ½-inch ribbons

Kosher salt

4 tablespoons (½ stick) unsalted butter, at room temperature

4 ounces soft goat cheese

3 tablespoons fresh tarragon leaves, or 2 teaspoons dried

8 boneless, skin-on chicken thighs, pounded ¼ inch thick by your butcher

Freshly ground black pepper

2½ cups panko bread crumbs

2 large eggs

1 teaspoon whole milk

½ cup all-purpose flour

1 quart virgin olive oil

In a 12-inch sauté pan, heat the ¼ cup of oil over medium heat. Add the garlic and sauté until light brown, about 1 minute, then add the kale and 1 teaspoon salt and cook, stirring regularly, until the kale is fully cooked, gray–olive green, and very tender, 10 to 12 minutes. Remove and allow to cool completely. Place the cooled kale in a food processor, add the butter, goat cheese, and tarragon, and process until smooth. Transfer to a bowl and chill for 30 minutes.

Lay eight 10-inch-long pieces of plastic wrap on the counter, separately.

Lay 1 chicken thigh on each piece of plastic wrap, season with salt and pepper, and place 1½ tablespoons of the kale-butter and 1 tablespoon of the panko in the center of each piece. Using the plastic wrap to assist, fold in the ends of the thigh and roll, completely enclosing the kale-butter mixture. Roll very tightly in the plastic to create an impermeable log. Keep in mind that any loose edge will allow the kale mixture to leak out, so be very attentive. Repeat with each thigh. Place the wrapped thighs in the refrigerator for 2 hours, or up to overnight.

Place the eggs and milk in a flat bowl and whisk to combine. Place the flour and a pinch of salt and pepper in another flat bowl. Place the remaining 2 cups panko in a third bowl with 2 tablespoons salt.

Heat 2 inches of oil in a Dutch oven or a high-sided sauté pan over medium-high heat until it registers 375°F on a deep-fry thermometer.

Remove the chicken from the plastic wrap. Dip each thigh into the flour mixture, shaking off any excess. Dip the thighs into the egg mixture, letting any excess drip off, then roll in the panko. Gently place each thigh in the hot oil, sealed side down, and cook until golden brown, 6 to 8 minutes on each side, until the internal temperature registers 165°F on a meat thermometer. Transfer to a wire rack set on a rimmed baking sheet and allow to drain for a minute before serving. If not serving immediately, you can hold the chicken in a preheated 300°F oven for up to 30 minutes.

BRAISED CHICKEN

with Sautéed Apples and Prosecco

Cooking in wine adds delicate acidity and delightful grapey sweetness to the final dish. That dulcet tone is echoed in the nearly caramel flavor of the apples in their vinegary sweet-and-sour bath.

SERVES 4

FOR THE CHICKEN

¼ cup extra-virgin olive oil

1 (3½-pound) broiler chicken, cut into 8 serving pieces, rinsed and patted dry

Kosher salt

1 large onion, cut into ½-inch dice

2 carrots, cut into 1-inch pieces

¼ cup raisins

2 cups prosecco or any dry white wine

FOR THE APPLES

2 tablespoons extra-virgin olive oil

2 Ginger Gold apples, or another tart apple, such as Granny Smith, peeled, cored, and cut into ½-inch-thick slices

2 cloves garlic, grated on a Microplane

3 tablespoons red wine vinegar

3 tablespoons sugar

2 tablespoons chopped fresh chives

1 teaspoon poppy seeds

TO ASSEMBLE

1 bunch fresh flat-leaf parsley, finely chopped (¼ cup)

Extra-virgin olive oil, for drizzling

MAKE THE CHICKEN

In a 10- to 12-inch sauté pan, heat the olive oil over high heat until very hot but not smoking. Season the chicken with salt and place it in the pan, skin side down. Brown the chicken on both sides, 6 to 8 minutes per side, and transfer the pieces to a plate as they are finished. Reduce the heat to medium, add the onion and carrots, and cook, stirring, until deep golden brown. Add the raisins to the pan and stir well. Add the wine and bring to a boil. Return the chicken to the pan, cover, reduce the heat to maintain a simmer, and cook for 30 minutes, or until the chicken is cooked through.

MAKE THE APPLES

In a 12-inch sauté pan, heat the olive oil over medium-high heat until smoking. Add the apples and garlic and cook, quickly stirring and shaking the pan continuously, until the apples have just softened and are nicely browned. Add the vinegar and sugar and cook, tossing continuously, until the mixture has reduced to a syrup. Remove from the heat and set aside in a warm place. Stir in the chives and the poppy seeds.

ASSEMBLE THE DISH

Transfer the chicken to a warmed platter and stir the parsley into the liquid remaining in the pan. Spoon the sauce over the chicken. Drizzle with olive oil and serve with the apples, spooned over each piece tableside.

Nashville

Chef:
ERIK ANDERSON, THE CATBIRD SEAT

Farmer:
KAREN OVERTON, WEDGE OAK FARM

Ingredient:
CHICKEN

DAY 60: *Somewhere in the middle of a seven-course meal at The Catbird Seat in Nashville, Chef Erik Anderson delivers a dish he calls Chicken and Pasta. It sounds simple, but don't be fooled.*

The flavors are deep and rich. The chicken is perfectly tender. We want to know more.

Erik describes the dish as a chicken breast encrusted in salt and indigenous Tennessee spices, then roasted. The crust is removed and the breast roasted again, this time in Wagyu beef fat. There are featherlight gnocchi made with local sheep's milk cheese, roasted candy onions, charred leek hearts, and a luscious potato broth spiked with country ham.

He says the chicken is from Wedge Oak Farm in Lebanon, Tennessee, about thirty miles away, where Karen Overton raises the poultry and eggs Erik serves at The Catbird Seat.

That's a start. Now we want to know the whole story. To get it, we have to go back almost two months.

DAY 3: There are 311 Cornish Cross chicks in a stall of a century-old barn at Wedge Oak Farm. They had arrived at the post office earlier in the day, two days after hatching in Iowa.

So there is no riddle: At Wedge Oak, the chickens came first.

The farm was built by Karen's great-grandparents, but how it got its name is a mystery: As far as anyone can tell, there is no tree called a wedge oak.

Karen and her siblings moved away to careers in New York, Boston, and Birmingham. In 2008, her parents said they were thinking about selling parts of the farm, and none of the other kids seemed interested in taking over.

But Karen was. She had worked around the world as an archaeologist and an art fabricator, and she was ready to come home to the farm.

But back to our chicks.

The puffs of fluff are, for reasons that track with logic, not much larger than an egg. They are kept warm and safe. They're hungry, and are fed food high in protein to help develop bones and organs, infrastructure that will support the muscle they'll later be encouraged to grow.

At this stage, the chickens are impossibly cute and perpetually bouncy. It's easy to see how they became an icon of spring.

This stage doesn't last long.

DAY 6: The chicks have increased their initial body weight by about fifty percent in seventy-two hours. They're less tiny, but still pretty cute.

DAY 19: The flock has reached an awkward teenage stage. All of them are noticeably larger, though many seem as if their necks and legs didn't

get the same memo on how fast to grow.

DAY 33: Any cuteness is pretty much gone. The birds have the general structure of a chicken but haven't developed the stately look of a thickly feathered laying hen. They never will. There's no more bouncing. They walk around briskly, but haven't acquired a signature cocky strut.

Coats of feathers are coming in, and that's a rite of passage: As soon as the feathers are full, the birds can go to the pasture. They're now on a low-protein diet, eating more and building muscle. Muscle means meat.

While in the barn, the chickens get to listen to the radio. Karen found that a steady stream of NPR keeps predators from trying to get in, and the chickens seem to like it.

At least until *Prairie Home Companion* comes on. The chickens hate that, Karen says. She might be joking. Either way, there's a jazz station to fill the gap.

Once they move to the pasture, the chickens are free to strut around and eat all the bugs, grubs, and worms they can find to supplement their feed.

There is some bad news for the chickens, which now weigh a little less than two pounds each: Some chefs like small birds. These chickens are fair game.

DAY 47: A deluge that flooded a field and caused Karen to bring the chickens back to the barn has passed, and the pasture is recovering. The chickens are hauled back out, where they join the laying flock.

Eggs are big business. Karen knows that no matter how many eggs she takes to market, she probably won't bring any home.

Among yardbirds, being a laying hen is a good gig. Not only do they stay around longer—two years instead of two months—but there's a lot of diversity. Breeds include Araucana, Barred Rock, Rhode Island Red, Tetra Tint, and Black Giant. There's an array of color, among both the birds in the pasture and the eggs in the carton.

And the food's good. Erik shows his appreciation by bringing the chickens oyster shells from the restaurant.

Pecking at those provides an added source of calcium, which is good for egg production.

DAY 58: The broilers have lived a life protected from the elements and predators, well fed and with room to move.

But tomorrow isn't going to be a great day.

In late afternoon, almost two hundred birds go into crates and onto the trailer behind Karen's truck. A crate is designed to hold sixteen birds, but she puts eight or nine birds in each so they'll be a little more comfortable.

One bird in the bunch looks a little scrawny, and Karen considers giving him a two-week reprieve. But by then, he'll be a giant. A small bird is more attractive to customers than one that's too big.

He goes on the truck.

DAY 59: It isn't 5 a.m. yet, and the roosters are already sounding the alarm—business as usual.

Of course, the roosters aren't going anywhere.

Karen drives her trailer full of chickens 85 miles to an organic processing plant, where she spends the day as her birds are dispatched, cleaned, processed, inspected, chilled, and packaged.

She could drop the birds off, go home, and pick them up tomorrow, avoiding the unpleasantness. But Karen feels a sense of duty to the birds. They're fulfilling a "specific errand," she says, and she has one, too: to make the lives of her birds happy and healthy, and their sacrifice respectful.

After eight hours at the plant, the crates are empty, her coolers are full, and Karen heads home.

DAY 60: Karen's chickens are delivered to restaurants around Nashville. At The Catbird Seat, a salt-and-spice crust awaits.

STUFFED TURKEY

with Apples and Walnuts

Apples, walnuts, and sausage together are a kind of holy trinity in poultry cooking, and when married to sage and lots of nutmeg, the trinity becomes magical. You'll see.

SERVES 8 TO 12

1 (5- to 6-pound) whole turkey breast, boned, halved, and butterflied by your butcher

Kosher salt

2 tablespoons freshly ground black pepper, plus more as needed

3 tablespoons plus ¼ cup extra-virgin olive oil

1 pound turkey sausage

2 apples, peeled, cored, and cut into ½-inch dice

½ cup walnut pieces

2 cups panko bread crumbs

½ cup freshly grated Parmigiano-Reggiano

2 large eggs

1 teaspoon freshly grated nutmeg

1 tablespoon chopped fresh sage leaves

1 bunch fresh flat-leaf parsley, finely chopped (¼ cup)

2 cups dry white wine

2 cups chicken broth

Pound the butterflied turkey breast halves to flatten them, then season with salt and pepper and refrigerate.

Preheat the oven to 400°F.

In a 12- to 14-inch sauté pan, heat 3 tablespoons of the olive oil over medium heat until smoking. Add the turkey sausage and cook, breaking it up with a wooden spoon as it cooks, until golden brown, 7 to 9 minutes. Drain all but 4 tablespoons of the fat from the pan and add the apples and walnut pieces. Cook for 8 minutes, or until the apples soften. Remove from the heat and allow to cool for 20 minutes. Add the panko, Parmigiano, eggs, 2 tablespoons of pepper, the nutmeg, and herbs and stir with your hands, as you would for meatloaf or burgers, just until it comes together.

Place the two turkey pieces on a cutting board, skin side down, and divide the stuffing between them. Roll each of the breasts like a jelly roll and tie them firmly in several places with butcher's twine. Place the two rolls on a rack set in a roasting pan, skin side up. Pour 1 cup of the wine and 1 cup of the broth over them, season with salt and pepper, and roast until they are dark golden brown on the outside and a meat thermometer inserted into the fattest part of the breast registers 165°F, about 1 hour, plus or minus 10 minutes. Remove the pan from the oven, place the turkey rolls on a cutting board, and let them rest for 15 minutes before carving.

Place the roasting pan on the stovetop over medium-high heat. Add the remaining 1 cup wine and 1 cup broth to the pan and deglaze, scraping the bottom of the pan with a wooden spoon. Cook for 5 minutes, then add the remaining ¼ cup oil. Shake the pan to emulsify the sauce and season with salt and pepper.

Carve the turkey rolls into ½-inch slices and drizzle with the pan sauce.

TEXAS RED FLANNEL HASH

with Fried Eggs

SERVES 6

2 large bunches beets

2 tablespoons olive oil

2 pounds waxy golden potatoes, such as Yukon Gold (4 medium or 2 large), cut in half

2 tablespoons kosher salt, plus more as needed

7 tablespoons unsalted butter

2 dried ancho chiles, soaked in hot water for 10 minutes

1 pound cooked corned beef, cut into ¼-inch dice (you may substitute any leftover protein)

Freshly ground black pepper

2 tablespoons Worcestershire sauce

1 bunch fresh cilantro, finely chopped

6 extra-large eggs

Texas Pete hot sauce, for serving

This is a Yankee dish that makes sense in Texas if you add some chiles, which render it completely nontraditional. Hash was originally created by crafty chefs to use up leftovers, but merits first use as it is so delicious and really belts out flavor in the key of beets. You can easily substitute roast turkey or pork or any other kind of cooked meat to personalize this dish.

Preheat the oven to 450°F.

Cut off the beet greens and reserve them for ravioli filling or soup. Scrub the beets, toss them with 1 tablespoon of the olive oil, and spread them in a baking pan. Roast until very tender, 50 to 60 minutes. Let cool slightly, then rub off the skins under running water. Cut into ¼-inch dice and set aside.

Place the potatoes in a saucepan, cover with cold water, and add 2 tablespoons salt. Bring to a boil and cook until tender, about 20 minutes. Peel, cut into ¼-inch dice, and set aside.

In a 12-inch cast-iron skillet, melt 6 tablespoons of the butter over medium-high heat. Split the ancho chiles and remove the seeds, then cut them into thin strips and add them to the pan with the beets, potatoes, and corned beef and season with salt and pepper. Toss and cook until heated through, about 10 minutes. Add the Worcestershire and cilantro and reduce the heat to low. Once the hash is crispy, turn off the heat and let it set for 5 to 10 minutes. This will help to keep it together when slicing.

Meanwhile, in a 12-inch nonstick pan, heat the remaining 1 tablespoon butter and 1 tablespoon olive oil over medium heat. Once it has foamed and subsided, crack the eggs into the pan, season with salt and pepper, and fry to the desired doneness.

Serve the hash, topping each portion with a fried egg, with Texas Pete hot sauce on the side.

PORK LOIN ROAST

with Fresh Sauerkraut "Quick-Style"

This pork roast is the perfect Sunday supper in the fall, when fresh cabbages abound in the market. If you do not plan ahead or have the time to make fresh sauerkraut, the bagged kraut in the refrigerated section of your grocery store is excellent.

SERVES 6

1 tablespoon kosher salt

1 tablespoon freshly ground black pepper

1 tablespoon fennel seeds

4 cloves garlic, finely chopped

8 fresh sage leaves, chopped, or 2 tablespoons dried sage

Several gratings of nutmeg

3 cups fresh sauerkraut (recipe below)

1 (3-pound) pork loin on the bone

3 tablespoons plus ¼ cup extra-virgin olive oil

Preheat the oven to 400°F.

In a small bowl, combine the salt, pepper, fennel seeds, garlic, sage, and nutmeg and stir well to combine. Place the sauerkraut in an oven-proof casserole and place the pork loin on top. Rub the salt-and-spice mixture all over the loin. Drizzle 3 tablespoons of the olive oil over the loin and roast for 1 hour 10 minutes, or until a meat thermometer inserted into the center registers 145°F.

Allow the meat to rest for 10 minutes before carving. Serve with pan juices and sauerkraut and drizzled with the remaining ¼ cup oil.

2 tablespoons extra-virgin olive oil

1 medium onion, thinly sliced

1 teaspoon caraway seeds

1 head green cabbage, cut into ½-inch ribbons

1 cup apple cider vinegar

½ cup apple cider

1 cup hard cider

2 tablespoons kosher salt

FRESH SAUERKRAUT "QUICK-STYLE"

Heat the oil in a Dutch oven or high-sided pan over medium-high heat. Add the onion and caraway and sauté until soft, about 6 minutes.

Add the cabbage, vinegar, cider, hard cider, and salt and bring to a boil. Cover, reduce the heat, and simmer for about 30 minutes, or until the cabbage is tender.

This can be kept in an airtight container in the fridge for up to 2 weeks.

MAKES 2 QUARTS

BRAISED PORK BELLY

with Black Beans, Marielito-Style

This dish celebrates the flavors of the Cuban immigrant kitchen and takes a little time, but is totally worth it for the ultimate expression of porcine succulence.

SERVES 6

FOR THE RUB AND PORK BELLY

½ cup brown sugar

2 tablespoons fennel seeds, toasted and ground

3 tablespoons kosher salt

3 tablespoons finely chopped rosemary

1 tablespoon red pepper flakes

3 pounds pork belly, skin removed

FOR THE BRAISE

3 tablespoons extra-virgin olive oil

3 carrots, cut into ½-inch pieces

4 ribs celery, cut into ½-inch pieces

1 red onion, sliced

2 leeks, trimmed 2 inches from the end, cut into ½-inch half-moons and washed well

1 tablespoon celery seeds

1 bottle of your favorite beer

Kosher salt

2 tablespoons honey

FOR THE BLACK BEANS

2 (15-ounce) cans black beans, drained and rinsed

½ red onion, sliced

¼ cup fresh mint, chopped

¼ cup fresh basil leaves, chopped

2 jalapeños, cut into ¼-inch dice

2 tablespoons apple cider vinegar

Kosher salt and freshly ground black pepper

5 scallions, very thinly sliced

MAKE THE RUB AND MARINATE THE PORK BELLY

Combine all the ingredients except for the pork belly in a small bowl and very thoroughly mix them. Using a sharp knife, score a 1-inch grid pattern into the fat of the pork belly. Rub the pork belly all over with the spice mixture and refrigerate overnight or at least 2 hours.

BRAISE THE PORK BELLY

Preheat the oven to 350°F.

In a large Dutch oven, heat the olive oil over medium-high heat. Sear the pork, fat side down, until light brown and crispy. Keep an eye on it, as it can overdarken in this step. Take your time—it should take 10 to 12 minutes. Flip the pork and brown the other side. When it is golden brown, transfer the pork to a platter.

Add the carrots, celery, red onion, leeks, celery seeds, and beer to the Dutch oven and season with salt. Bring to a boil, return the pork belly to the pot, and push it to submerge halfway in the liquid. Place the pot in the oven and cook, uncovered, for 2 hours.

MAKE THE BLACK BEANS

While the pork is cooking, place the beans in a bowl with the red onion, mint, basil, jalapeños, and cider vinegar, season with salt and pepper, and gently stir to mix well, then set aside.

ASSEMBLE THE DISH

Transfer the pork belly gently to a large cutting board and brush with the honey. Pour off half the rendered fat. Add the bean mixture to the braising liquid, stir, and simmer over medium heat for about 10 minutes. Place the bean-and-vegetable mixture on a platter. Cut the pork belly into ½-inch-thick slices and arrange them over the beans. Sprinkle with sliced scallions and serve.

PORCHETTA, SPICY FLORIDA-STYLE

SERVES 6 TO 8

1 (4-pound) boneless pork shoulder, with the fat on

Kosher salt

Freshly ground black pepper

¼ cup extra-virgin olive oil

1 medium red onion, cut into ¼-inch dice

1 bunch kale, thinly sliced

2 fresh chorizo sausages, casings removed

2 tablespoons fennel seeds

1 tablespoon ground cumin

10 cloves garlic, thinly sliced

2 bunches fresh flat-leaf parsley, finely chopped (½ cup)

2 large eggs, beaten

3 tablespoons fennel pollen or ground fennel seeds

8 carrots, scrubbed

1 cup dry white wine, such as Frascati

The traditional seasoning of fennel is present in this "Floribbean" version of the Tuscan classic, but the cumin and the chorizo create something quite magical to this trance-inducer. I guarantee that you will be carried out of the kitchen like a winning Super Bowl coach every time you serve this dish; it is a franchise player.

Preheat the oven to 350°F.

Have your butcher butterfly the pork shoulder to an even 1-inch thickness; you should have a flat piece of meat about 8 inches by 14 inches. Sprinkle with salt and pepper and set aside.

In a sauté pan, heat the olive oil until smoking. Add the onion and kale and sauté until the onion is softened and lightly browned, about 8 minutes. Add the chorizo, fennel seeds, cumin, garlic, and 2 tablespoons of pepper, and cook until the mixture assumes a light color, stirring continuously, about 10 minutes. Remove from the heat and allow to cool. Add the parsley and eggs and mix well.

Spread the mixture over the pork, roll it up like a jelly roll, and score the fat on the outside in a 2-inch diamond pattern. Sprinkle aggressively with salt and sprinkle the fennel pollen all over, rubbing to get it into the crevices. Tie with butcher's twine and place in a roasting pan on top of the carrots, kind of like a roasting rack. Roast for 2 hours, then open the oven and pour the wine over the porchetta and baste with the drippings. Close the oven and roast for 45 minutes to 1 hour more, until the internal temperature registers 175°F on a meat thermometer. Remove and allow to rest for 15 to 20 minutes. Slice into 1-inch-thick pieces and serve with the whole carrots from the roasting pan.

PORK SHANKS

with Parsnips and Maple

This dish is a Sunday supper, a showstopper, and a party all rolled into one.

SERVES 6 TO 8

4 (1½- to 2-pound) fresh pork foreshanks

Kosher salt and freshly ground black pepper

½ cup rye flour

¼ cup olive oil

2 yellow onions, cut into ½-inch dice

2 ribs celery, cut into ¼-inch dice

2 carrots, halved lengthwise and cut into ¼-inch half-moons

6 parsnips, peeled and cut into 1-inch pieces

4 cloves garlic, thinly sliced

1 (6-ounce) can tomato paste

2 tablespoons chopped fresh thyme

3 cups chicken stock

1 cup sweet Riesling

½ cup plus 2 tablespoons pure, grade A maple syrup

2 bunches fresh chives, thinly sliced

1 lemon

1 (½-pound) piece fresh horseradish, peeled and grated, or 1 cup prepared horseradish

Preheat the oven to 375°F.

Season the pork shanks with salt and pepper. Dredge the shanks in the flour, shaking off the excess.

In a large braising pot, heat the olive oil over medium-high heat until just smoking. Add the shanks and brown on all sides, 12 to 15 minutes total. Transfer to a plate.

Add the onions, celery, carrots, and parsnips to the pan and cook, stirring occasionally, until just tender, 6 minutes. Add the garlic, tomato paste, and thyme and cook for 1 minute. Stir in the stock, wine, and ½ cup of the maple syrup and bring the mixture to a boil. Return the shanks to the pan, cover, and transfer to the oven. Bake, turning the shanks every 45 minutes, until the meat is fork-tender and almost falls off the bone, 2½ to 3 hours. Remove the shanks from the braising liquid and transfer to an ovenproof platter. Reduce the oven temperature to 200°F and return the shanks to the oven to keep warm.

Skim the fat off the braising liquid, set the pan over medium-high heat, and bring to a boil, then immediately reduce the heat to maintain a simmer and cook until the liquid has thickened, 20 to 25 minutes. Stir in half of the chives and taste for seasoning. Garnish the shanks with some of the sauce, then top with the remaining chives and drizzle the remaining 2 tablespoons maple syrup over. Halve the lemon and squeeze the juice over the whole shebang. Serve immediately with fresh horseradish and the remaining braising juices.

PORK CHOPS

with Peppers and Capers

SERVES 4

2 cups water

1 cup kosher salt, plus more as needed

1 cup packed brown sugar

12 whole black peppercorns

4 bay leaves

4 quarts cold water

4 pork single-bone rib chops, about 1¼ inches thick

3 tablespoons plus ¼ cup extra-virgin olive oil

3 red bell peppers, seeded and cut into thin strips

3 yellow bell peppers, seeded and cut into thin strips

2 red onions, cut into ½-inch dice

¼ cup Gaeta olives, pitted

1 teaspoon red pepper flakes

1 cup dry white wine

2 tablespoons small capers, with their brine

8 pickled hot cherry peppers

Freshly ground black pepper

4 scallions, thinly sliced

We always use a brine for pork chops, and sometimes for larger cuts of pork as well. Brining the chops before grilling them guarantees succulent meat even when cooked to medium-well. The piquant, spicy combo of red and yellow peppers, red pepper flakes, and capers makes this dish feel and taste like a bit of San Gennaro.

In a small saucepan, combine 2 cups of water, 1 cup of salt, and the brown sugar and heat over high heat, stirring, until the salt and sugar dissolve. Pour the brine into a large, deep bowl or other container large enough to hold the pork and the brine. Add the peppercorns, bay leaves, and 4 quarts of cold water and stir to mix well.

Make sure the brine is completely cool, then add the pork chops. Cover and let stand for at least 2 hours, or refrigerate overnight. Do not brine the pork for longer than 12 hours, or it will get a little pickled.

In a large pot, heat 3 tablespoons of the olive oil over high heat until smoking. Add the bell peppers, onions, olives, and red pepper flakes and cook, without stirring, for about 5 minutes, until the peppers and onions are slightly charred. Stir a couple of times and then cook for 5 minutes more. Add the wine and capers and bring to a boil. Add the whole pickled cherry peppers, then reduce the heat to maintain a simmer and cook for 10 minutes. Season with salt and black pepper, remove from the heat, and set aside.

Heat a cast-iron or other heavy-bottomed skillet over medium-high heat.

Drain the chops and pat dry with paper towels. Season both sides with salt and black pepper. Brush the chops with the remaining ¼ cup olive oil, place them into the skillet, and cook, without moving them, for 6 minutes. Turn the chops over and cook for 5 minutes more, or until they register 135°F on a meat thermometer. Pour the pepper mixture into the pan and over the chops and bring to a sizzling boil. Reduce the heat to medium-low and simmer for 10 minutes, basting and moving the pepper mixture to warm it through.

Transfer the chops to a platter, stir the scallions into the pepper mixture, and spoon the pepper mixture over the chops. Arrange 2 cherry peppers on top of each chop and serve.

VEAL BRACIOLE

My Grandma Called "Coietti"

SERVES 6

1½ pounds veal hip or shoulder

Leaves from 4 bunches fresh flat-leaf parsley (4 cups)

1 cup freshly grated Pecorino Romano, plus more for serving

1 teaspoon freshly grated nutmeg

Coarse sea salt and freshly ground black pepper

1 cup all-purpose flour, for dredging

¼ cup extra-virgin olive oil, plus more for drizzling

1 cup dry white wine

1½ cups Basic Tomato Sauce (page 145)

1 bunch fresh oregano, for strewing

Red pepper flakes, for serving

This was a special treat dish from the LaFramboise side of the family—apparently they learned it from an Italian family in Roslyn, Washington, a generation back. My dad still makes it for the family every time he and Mom come to visit New York City. It is a case of better ingredients making a much better dish, so find some nice veal—it will improve your life.

Have your butcher cut the veal into 12 thin scallops and pound them to a consistent flatness—about ¼ inch thick.

In a bowl, combine the parsley, cheese, and nutmeg and stir until well blended.

Season the meat with coarse salt and then divide the parsley mixture evenly over the veal, spreading it to form a thin layer on top of each piece.

Roll up each piece like a jelly roll and tie securely with two pieces of butcher's twine. Season the outside of the rolls with salt and black pepper. Place the flour in a shallow bowl and dredge the rolled veal in the flour.

In a 12- to 14-inch skillet, heat the olive oil over medium-high heat until almost smoking. Place the rolls in the pan in batches of 6 and brown the rolls for 8 to 10 minutes, turning them every 2 to 3 minutes, until deeply caramelized and browned. Transfer the browned rolls to a plate and set aside. Drain the excess fat from the skillet and add fresh olive oil, if necessary, then brown the remaining 6 rolls.

Drain most of the juices from the pan. Add the white wine and tomato sauce and bring to a boil, then return the veal rolls to the pan and simmer for about 10 minutes, or until the veal is just cooked through and the sauce is glossy and has the consistency of a thin gravy. The rolls should have an internal temperature of about 135°F. Sprinkle with fresh oregano, then place on a platter.

Serve with red pepper flakes, a drizzle of oil over each roll, and Pecorino on the side.

GRILLED SKIRT STEAK

with Cherry Barbecue Sauce

Perhaps my fave steak of all for flavor and bang for the buck, skirt steak loves a marinade and longs to be cut against the grain. Using Dr Pepper in the barbecue sauce is a trick I learned in my NASCAR world, and it will surprise you!

SERVES 4

FOR THE STEAK

¼ cup fresh rosemary leaves, finely chopped, plus 4 sprigs for serving

2 tablespoons juniper berries, crushed

1 bunch fresh oregano, finely chopped

4 cloves garlic, finely chopped

½ cup extra-virgin olive oil

2 pounds skirt steak, cleaned of the fat cap and sinew

FOR THE BARBECUE SAUCE

¼ cup extra-virgin olive oil

1 medium onion, chopped

2 jalapeños, chopped

2 tablespoons ancho chile powder

2 (6-ounce) cans tomato paste

1 (12-ounce) can Dr Pepper

Zest and juice of 2 oranges

¼ cup packed brown sugar

1 cup frozen tart cherries

¼ cup red wine vinegar

TO ASSEMBLE

Kosher salt and freshly cracked black pepper

1 tablespoon ancho chile powder

MAKE THE STEAK

In a 1-gallon zip-top bag, combine the chopped rosemary, juniper, oregano, garlic, and olive oil, seal the bag, and shake well to blend. Place the steak in the bag and massage to coat with the herb mixture. Seal the bag and refrigerate for at least 4 hours or overnight.

MAKE THE BARBECUE SAUCE

In a medium saucepan, heat the olive oil over medium heat until smoking. Add the onion, jalapeños, and chile powder and cook until softened, about 8 minutes. Add the tomato paste and cook for 3 minutes, then add the Dr Pepper, orange zest, orange juice, sugar, and cherries. Bring the mixture to a boil, then reduce the heat to maintain a simmer and cook, stirring frequently, for 10 minutes more.

Transfer the mixture to a blender or a food processor fitted with the metal blade, add the vinegar, and blend until smooth. Transfer to a plastic container and set aside until ready to serve. (If you're not using it immediately, the barbecue sauce can be stored in the fridge for up to 2 weeks.)

ASSEMBLE THE DISH

Preheat the grill or broiler.

Remove the steak from the marinade, brush off the marinade, and season aggressively with salt and pepper. Place the steak on the hottest part of the grill and cook for 4 minutes on one side, then turn carefully with tongs and cook for 2 minutes on the other side.

Remove the steak from the grill and let it rest for 3 minutes.

Place 2 tablespoons of the barbecue sauce in the center of each of four plates. Slice the steak on an angle about ¼ inch thick, against the grain, and divide the slices evenly among the plates in little piles on top of the sauce. Sprinkle each plate with some of the ancho chile powder and serve immediately, with a sprig of rosemary on the side of each plate.

BUTTERFLIED LEG OF LAMB

on the Grill with Homemade Apple-Mint Jelly

SERVES 6 TO 8

FOR THE APPLE-MINT JELLY

2 pounds Granny Smith apples, roughly chopped into 2-inch pieces, skin, seeds, and all

2 cups lightly packed fresh mint leaves, chopped

1 cup water

1 cup apple cider vinegar

1¾ cups sugar

¼ cup honey

FOR THE LAMB

¼ cup olive oil

1 cup dry red wine

2 bunches fresh oregano, roughly chopped

2 bunches scallions, finely chopped

12 cloves garlic, roughly chopped

2 tablespoons kosher salt, plus more for seasoning

1 tablespoon freshly ground black pepper

1 (4½- to 5-pound) boneless leg of lamb, butterflied and trimmed of excess fat (or one 7- to 8-pound bone-in leg, boned, butterflied, and trimmed)

12 (1-inch-long) fresh rosemary sprigs, plus more leaves for serving

I love lamb on the grill, and using a butterflied leg gives me the best ratio of crisp, charred outside to pink-tender inside of any lamb dish I know. The mint jelly can be made in a larger batch and will last all winter long if you carefully can it (go to usda.gov and search for "canning"). Make the jelly and marinate the lamb the day before you plan on serving this.

MAKE THE APPLE-MINT JELLY

In a large pan, combine the apples, mint, and water. Bring to a boil, then reduce the heat to maintain a simmer, and cook for 20 minutes, until the apples are soft.

Add the vinegar, return the mixture to a boil, cover with a lid, and simmer for 10 minutes.

Using a potato masher, mash up the apple pieces to the consistency of applesauce. Spoon the apple mash and all of the liquid into a fine strainer and suspend over a large bowl. Set aside to drain for several hours. Do not squeeze. Note that if your mash is too thick, you can add ½ cup to 1 cup more water to it. You should have 2 cups of juice in the bowl when the mash has been drained.

Pour the juice into a large pot. Add the sugar and the honey, place over medium heat, and stir to dissolve, then bring to a boil and cook for 20 minutes. Skim off any scum that rises to the top as you go, then use a candy thermometer and heat the mixture to 225°F. Remove from the heat and pour into sterile jars. The jelly will need to be refrigerated overnight to set to my happy place. Any jelly you're not using immediately can be stored in the refrigerator for up to 4 weeks.

MAKE THE LAMB

Combine the olive oil, red wine, oregano, scallions, garlic, salt, and pepper in a small bowl and set aside.

Continued on page 226.

Make 12 small incisions in the fatty side of the lamb and insert one of the rosemary sprigs into each slit. Put the lamb in a large bowl or plastic container and pour the marinade over, turning to coat. Let stand at cool room temperature for at least 2 hours, or cover and refrigerate overnight; turn the lamb occasionally if you remember to.

If the lamb has been in the refrigerator, bring it to room temperature at least an hour before you are going to cook it.

Preheat a gas grill or prepare a fire in a charcoal grill.

Remove the lamb from the marinade, draining it well, and pat dry. Season all over with salt and place the lamb on the grill, fat side down. Grill until well charred on the first side. Turn and cook for 10 to 12 minutes more, or until well charred on the second side; the internal temperature should register 130°F on a meat thermometer for medium-rare. You will have to move the lamb every now and then if a flare-up happens; get into it, you are the master of the fire. Remove the lamb when perfectly cooked and transfer to a carving board. Let rest for 15 minutes.

Carve the lamb into ¼-inch-thick slices and serve immediately with rosemary leaves on top and the apple-mint jelly on the side.

TORTILLA ESPAÑOLA WITH PIMENTÓN

SERVES 4 AS A LIGHT DINNER WITH A NICE SALAD

¼ cup plus 3 tablespoons extra-virgin olive oil

1½ pounds baby fingerling potatoes, peeled and thinly sliced

1 medium Spanish onion, thinly sliced

1 teaspoon kosher salt, plus more as needed

1 teaspoon freshly ground black pepper, plus more as needed

8 extra-large eggs

1 tablespoon sweet pimentón

There is probably nothing that captures the pure flavor of a Spanish tapas bar like a well-made Spanish tortilla. This is the place where you can truly taste the difference between grocery store and farm-bought eggs and potatoes, so be sure to search out the very best you can find. Weiser's small silky fingerlings transform this warhorse into a masterpiece. I jacked it up a bit with smoky pimentón, but you can leave it out if you are a purist.

In a 10-inch cast-iron skillet (or a nonstick pan), heat ¼ cup of the oil over medium-high heat until smoking. Add the potatoes and onion, and season with salt and pepper. Reduce the heat to medium and cook slowly, tossing the pan and adjusting the heat if necessary so that the onions do not brown, until the potatoes are tender, 12 to 15 minutes. Transfer the potatoes and onions to a bowl. Lightly wipe the pan with a paper towel and place back over medium heat.

In a large bowl, beat the eggs with 1 teaspoon salt, 1 teaspoon pepper, and pimentón. Add the cooked potato mixture to the eggs and gently mix. Pour the remaining 3 tablespoons oil into the pan, then pour the potato-egg mixture in, spreading the potatoes evenly. Cook for about 1 minute, just to set the bottom of the egg mixture. Reduce the heat to medium-low and cook for 15 to 20 minutes, or until almost set throughout. Place a plate over the pan, carefully invert it, then slide the tortilla back into the pan, bottom side up, and cook for 4 to 5 minutes more until set. Flip out onto a clean plate, let rest for 10 minutes, and serve warm or at room temperature.

ACORN SQUASH

Stuffed with Lamb and Mint

The classic diner-special dish of stuffed peppers was the inspiration here, and the lamb is the protagonist that really echoes the sweetness of the squash much better than beef would.

SERVES 4 TO 6 AS A MAIN DISH OR 8 TO 10 AS A SIDE DISH

4 to 6 small to medium acorn squash, 1 to 1¼ pounds each

Sea salt and freshly ground black pepper

2 tablespoons extra-virgin olive oil

4 to 6 tablespoons commercial-grade balsamic vinegar

1 pound ground lamb

1 medium red onion, cut into ¼-inch dice

1 bulb fennel, cut into ¼-inch dice, fronds reserved

1 medium parsnip, peeled and thinly sliced into rounds

1 tablespoon ground cumin

½ cup red wine

2 cups cooked stelline or orzo pasta

1 cup loosely packed fresh mint leaves

¼ cup freshly grated Pecorino Romano

Preheat the oven to 450°F.

Cut ½ inch off the top of each acorn squash, reserving the tops, and scoop out the seeds. Carefully trim off a small slice from the bottoms of the squash so they'll sit flat in the pan. Season the inside of each squash with salt and pepper and rub the insides with olive oil and 1 tablespoon each balsamic vinegar. Place in a baking dish that will hold them relatively upright and set aside.

Place a 10- to 12-inch sauté pan over medium heat, and brown the lamb until no longer pink. Remove the meat from the pan and place in a bowl, leaving the fat behind, then add the onion, fennel, parsnip, and cumin to the pan and cook until quite soft, 8 to 10 minutes. Add the wine, stir to remove any slightly stuck bits from the bottom of the pan, and cook until reduced by half, just nice and moist.

Add the cooked vegetables, the cooked pasta, and the mint leaves to the lamb; stir gently to mix, and season with salt and pepper. Divide the mixture evenly among the squash. Sprinkle the tops with the Pecorino Romano, then top each squash with its lid and bake for 1 hour, or until the squash is tender. Remove and serve immediately.

BEEF AND CHARD MEATBALLS

The chard makes these meatballs so moist and tender that you will wonder, like I did, how it has escaped you all this time. If I do not tell anyone, they do not notice the chard, but instead exclaim over the dish's deliciousness. This is a game-changer both for texture and for lightening up a dish.

SERVES 4

FOR THE MEATBALLS

¼ cup extra-virgin olive oil

1 medium red onion, halved and cut into ⅓-inch-thick slices

3 cloves garlic, thinly sliced

1 pound Swiss chard, trimmed, stems and leaves cut into ¼-inch-thick slices

2 cups coarse fresh bread crumbs

1 pound ground beef chuck

1 pound turkey Italian sausage

½ cup whole milk

2 large eggs, lightly beaten

4 cloves garlic, grated on a Microplane

2 tablespoons chopped fresh marjoram

1 teaspoon red pepper flakes

2 tablespoons kosher salt, plus more as needed

2 tablespoons freshly ground black pepper, plus more as needed

FOR THE SAUCE

¼ cup extra-virgin olive oil

3 red onions, thinly sliced

6 cloves garlic, thinly sliced

1 tablespoon red pepper flakes

1 cup dry red wine

1 sprig fresh rosemary

2 cups Basic Tomato Sauce (page 145)

MAKE THE MEATBALLS

Preheat the oven to 475°F.

In a large sauté pan, heat the oil over medium-high heat. Stir in the onion and garlic. Add the Swiss chard and season with salt. Cover and cook for 5 minutes, or until the chard softens.

Toast the fresh bread crumbs in a dry pan until deep brown but not burned—watch them carefully to prevent burning. Set aside.

Uncover the chard, stir, and cook for 8 to 9 minutes more until the chard is very tender. Set aside to cool, then chop well and place between two plates to press out any liquid.

In a large bowl, combine the chard, beef, sausage, bread crumbs, milk, eggs, garlic, marjoram, red pepper flakes, salt, and black pepper and mix lightly with your hands until just combined. Form into golf ball–size meatballs and place in a shallow casserole.

Roast the meatballs until dark golden brown, about 15 minutes. Remove from the oven and reduce the oven temperature to 350°F.

MAKE THE SAUCE

In a large ovenproof skillet, heat the olive oil over high heat until smoking. Add the onions and garlic, reduce the heat to medium, and cook until well browned, about 5 minutes. Add the red pepper flakes, then the wine and rosemary, and bring to a boil. Cook until the wine has reduced by half. Add the tomato sauce and bring to a boil, then reduce the heat to maintain a simmer and cook for 15 minutes.

Add the meatballs to the sauce, place the pan in the oven, and bake for 1 hour.

Season the meatballs with salt and pepper. Serve in shallow bowls topped with the sauce.

Seven:
SIDE DISHES

CARROTS

with Cumin, Honey, and Ancho Chiles

This dish started as a side dish for Thanksgiving, but now I often serve it as a simple lunch or light supper with a bitter salad and a piece of ripe taleggio. These carrots are excellent either warm out of the pan or at room temperature.

SERVES 6 TO 8

2 tablespoons kosher salt, plus more as needed

12 medium carrots

½ cup red wine vinegar

1 ancho chile, chopped, with seeds

2 cloves garlic, thinly sliced

¼ cup extra-virgin olive oil

¼ cup honey

2 tablespoons cumin seeds

Bring 8 quarts of water to a boil in a pasta pot, and add 2 tablespoons salt. Add the carrots and boil until just tender, 5 to 6 minutes.

Meanwhile, in a 12-inch sauté pan, combine the vinegar, chile, garlic, oil, honey, cumin, and salt to taste and heat over low to medium-low heat.

Drain the carrots and, while still warm, transfer them to the pan with the honey mixture, toss to coat, and cook until the vinegar has evaporated and the carrots become sticky and shiny. Serve warm or at room temperature.

WARM POTATO SALAD

SERVES 6 TO 8

Kosher salt

3 pounds tiny new potatoes

¼ cup red wine vinegar

½ cup plus 1 tablespoon extra-virgin olive oil

3 extra-large eggs

¼ cup balsamic vinegar

1 tablespoon whole-grain mustard

3 tablespoons capers

Kosher salt and freshly ground pepper

Leaves from 1 bunch fresh marjoram

On a crisp autumn day at a tailgate party, or any winter afternoon involving sausages, there is almost nothing that pleases my family and our guests like a warm potato salad. I do the eggs sunny-side up and then slice them, which adds another layer of fun.

Bring a large pot of salted water to a boil. Add the potatoes and cook until just tender, 10 to 15 minutes. Drain and let the potatoes cool. Once the potatoes are cool enough to handle, slice them in half. Place them in a large bowl and while the spuds are still warm, add the red wine vinegar and toss gently to coat—the vinegar will all soak into the potatoes.

In a sauté pan, heat 1 tablespoon of the olive oil over medium heat and fry each egg, leaving the yolk soft-set and runny. Remove from the heat when cooked and thinly slice.

In a small bowl, combine the balsamic vinegar, mustard, capers, a pinch of salt and a few grinds of pepper, and whisk in the remaining ½ cup olive oil. Pour the mixture over the potatoes, then add the marjoram and the sliced eggs. Toss everything to coat, and serve warm.

If you need to make this in advance, do it all in the morning, then reheat in a 300°F oven for 30 minutes right before serving. Do not put this in the fridge if you do not have to; a chill will make the potatoes starchy.

YUKON GOLD MASHED POTATOES

There are many recipes for mashed potatoes, the most famous of which is Joel Robuchon's, with its equal parts potatoes, butter, and cream. I have always loved the spud more than the dairy, so mine are purely about the potatoes, with the oil and seasoning playing background.

SERVES 4 TO 6

2 pounds Yukon Gold potatoes, peeled and quartered

1 tablespoon kosher salt, plus more as needed

1 teaspoon freshly ground white pepper

½ teaspoon ground mace

½ cup of the best extra-virgin olive oil you can find

3 scallions, green and white parts thinly sliced

Place the potatoes in a large pot and add water to cover by 1 inch. Add a pinch of salt and bring to a boil. Simmer for 15 to 20 minutes, until the potatoes are fork-tender. Drain and pass the potatoes through a ricer or food mill into a large bowl. Season with 1 tablespoon salt, the white pepper, and the mace. Slowly drizzle in the olive oil, adding a bit then stirring to incorporate. Once all the oil is incorporated, add the scallions and stir through. Serve warm.

LATKES WITH CAVIAR

This is a mash-up of Russian "fancy" and Channukah supper and captures the celebratory spirit of the Festival of Lights. The most important step is the colander press; be sure to press very firmly to extract the water—it will guarantee a crisp crust for joyous crunchy happiness.

MAKES ABOUT 18 LATKES

1 large baking potato (1 pound), peeled

1 small Spanish onion

¼ cup rye flour

2 tablespoons matzo meal or crushed saltines

1 large egg, lightly beaten

2 teaspoons kosher salt

½ teaspoon freshly ground black pepper

Extra-virgin olive oil, for frying

1 cup sour cream

2 ounces of the best caviar you can afford (American paddlefish caviar is very good)

Coarsely shred the potato on the largest holes of a box grater. Grate the onion on the smaller holes. Place the potato and onion in a colander and press down firmly to extract the water. Let the mixture rest for 5 minutes and press again.

In a large bowl, whisk together the flour, matzo meal, egg, salt, and pepper. Stir in the potato-onion mixture until all the pieces are evenly coated.

In a medium skillet, heat 2 tablespoons of oil over medium-high heat until shimmering. Drop packed tablespoons of the potato mixture into the skillet and flatten them with a spatula. Cook the latkes until the edges are golden, about 2 minutes, then flip and cook until golden on the bottom, about 1 minute more. Drain on paper towels. Repeat with the remaining potato mixture, adding more oil to the skillet as needed. The key to getting the crispy edges is to press down on the latke only once, the very second it hits the pan, and then to let it cook long enough before the first turn.

Serve the sour cream and the caviar on the side, and let your guests place about 1 teaspoon of sour cream and ½ teaspoon of caviar on each latke.

ROMAN POTATO DOUGHNUTS

MAKES 20 DOUGHNUTS

1 pound Yukon Gold potatoes, peeled

1 (¼-ounce) package active dry yeast (2½ teaspoons)

1 cup warm buttermilk, 110° to 115°F

3 large eggs

5 tablespoons unsalted butter, melted

3 cups sugar

4 teaspoons baking powder

1½ teaspoons baking soda

1 teaspoon kosher salt

1 teaspoon freshly grated nutmeg

Zest of 2 oranges

5 cups all-purpose flour

4 cups olive oil, for frying, plus more for the bowl and baking sheet

I had always thought that the friggitoria culture was exclusive to Napoli and Campania, but I have recently discovered a few fry shops in Roma around the Trastevere part of town. After artichokes, my fave fried thing on my last trip was, oddly, the doughnuts called bomboloni di patate. *The spud brings it to another place texturally, adding a supreme creamy softness.*

Place the potatoes in a large pot, add water to cover, and bring to a boil. Boil gently until the potatoes are tender, 30 to 40 minutes. Drain and pass through a food mill or ricer into a large bowl. Let cool.

Meanwhile, sprinkle the yeast into the warm buttermilk, stir to dissolve, and let sit for 15 minutes, or until foamy.

To the potatoes, add the eggs, butter, 2 cups of the sugar, the baking powder, baking soda, salt, nutmeg, and orange zest and mix well to combine. Add the flour and the yeast mixture and knead well, about 5 minutes, then place in an oiled bowl, cover with a towel, and let the dough rise in a warm place for 1 hour, or until doubled in size.

Punch the dough down and turn it out onto a floured surface. Divide into 4 pieces and roll out each portion to ½-inch thickness. Cut with a floured 3-inch doughnut cutter, place each on an oiled baking sheet, cover with a towel, and let rise for 45 minutes, or until doubled in size.

In a deep pot, heat the olive oil over medium-high heat until it registers 375°F on a deep-fry thermometer. Line a plate with paper towels.

Working in batches, fry the doughnuts on one side about 3 minutes, then flip and fry for 1 to 2 minutes more, until golden brown all over. Remove with a slotted spoon and drain on the paper towel–lined plate.

Dust the doughnuts with the remaining 1 cup sugar, and serve warm.

Los Angeles

Chef:
MATT MOLINA, OSTERIA MOZZA

Farmer:
ALEX WEISER, WEISER FAMILY FARMS

Ingredient:
POTATOES

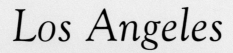
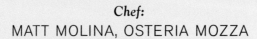

Some people can taste a wine and tell you the grape, where it's from, the year it was produced, whether it rained a lot that year.

Some people can taste a sauce and identify all its ingredients.

They've got nothing on Alex Weiser.

He's the face of Weiser Family Farms, a fixture at the farmers' markets around Los Angeles. And his face is familiar to the Southern California chefs who frequent those markets.

Alex orders a salad for lunch at one of those restaurants and goes to work.

He identifies the origins of each ingredient in rapid-fire: That comes from Barbara. Those are from James. That's from Phil. That's from Tutti Frutti. He does it so fast, you can't tell what came from whom.

They're the farmers who grew his lunch. They're his friends, colleagues, commiserators, and to some degree his competitors.

The chef here may have given the salad a name, but Alex gave it four.

Alex has spent more than three decades cultivating relationships in the food business. When he's in the city for markets, he goes to the restaurants that serve the food he grows. Chefs come to the markets to stock up and to catch up. They invite him to their events and cook at his.

One of the first chefs he met was Nancy Silverton. She told him what chefs want, and he listened. Through Nancy, he met Matt Molina, her chef at Osteria Mozza. Through Matt, he met Chad Colby, the chef at Chi Spacca. Farmers build a client base by word of mouth.

Alex sees a lot of similarity in the discipline of chefs and farmers. Both are driven by passion and dedication. Both work long hours. Both find themselves inspired by—or at the mercy of—the seasons. Both could do everything right and still go broke.

He loves providing the inspiration of a new vegetable and the challenge of delivering something rare and unique. He loves hearing chefs talk about vegetables they can't get, and telling them he'll grow it for them. He loves hearing them tell customers, "I have a farmer who grows this for me."

In the late 1970s, Sid Weiser was a high school teacher in Los Angeles. He always wanted to farm, so he retired and bought a 160-acre apple orchard in Tehachapi, two hours north of Los Angeles.

Then changes in California law allowed farmers to sell directly to the public. Farmers' markets started popping up, and Sid and his wife, Raquel, sent their son Alex into the city with boxes of apples to sell.

Those first markets looked nothing like the ones that line the streets around L.A. today. Customers went to markets to get things cheap, more like outlet shopping than picking through crates of pristine heirlooms. Local officials resisted markets then, not wanting traffic problems or competition for grocery stores.

Things have changed. Every city seems to have a market now. Or two. Customers are savvy and challenge chefs for the good stuff. Television crews showed up—this is L.A.—and the markets became tourist attractions.

The markets changed the neighborhoods. There were no high-end restaurants, upscale retailers, or glitzy movie houses along Santa Monica's Promenade when the market started there. Revitalization began with the market.

The Weisers' farm has changed, too. It now covers 350 acres in three cities. Alex's brother, Dan, and sister, Esther, joined the business, and nieces and a nephew are taking on responsibilities.

Alex heads to the city on big market days, but not because his crew needs him. He wants to be there. He goes to Santa Monica on Wednesdays and Saturdays, and Hollywood on Sundays.

Those are his days off.

"I'm here for the pleasure of it. This is the happiest place on earth."

Potatoes are the biggest crop at Weiser Family Farms. Fifty-five acres are planted with potatoes and each should yield about ten tons. Alex relays that statistic, thinks about it for a second, and does a double take.

That's a lot of potatoes. Maybe more than he realized.

His yield is huge, but his potatoes are small. The farm's old machinery harvested mature potatoes, the kind you get everywhere. Alex was walking through the field after a harvest and noticed all the small potatoes the harvester left. He started picking them up by hand. There were a lot. So he bought new machinery that wouldn't miss them.

Those baby fingerlings are now one of his most popular products. They're easy to cook. They have great flavor. They make a convenient serving size.

Small potatoes became big business.

Alex grows small celery root, too. Just not on purpose.

A chef was at the farm and spotted some smaller-than-average celery roots. He took them to his kitchen, loved them, declared Alex a genius for growing them, and asked for more.

The problem: Alex had no idea how he had done it. He knew he planted them late in the season. Maybe they grew slower during the shorter days?

Whatever it was, it wasn't a mistake; it's never a mistake if there's a success story in reach. He just learned there's a market for late-season celery root.

Then there's the story of how he learned there was a market for his bird bait.

Alex grew some berry bushes to keep birds out of his cash crops. For ten years, they worked like a champ. Then one day at the market, he saw Nancy buying berries from another farmer. She was paying a lot for them. And they looked familiar.

He'd been growing Persian mulberries, a delicacy, he learned. For the birds.

Now he grows them for pastry chefs.

As he finishes his salad, it's clear Alex isn't showing off or name-dropping. He's studying. He wants to know what chefs want—what they want *next*. He enjoys having a role in shaping menus. He respects that mistakes made at the farm today could create problems at his customers' restaurants in the coming months.

This was his parents' retirement project. Alex has been doing it for more than thirty years. Retirement isn't something he's thinking about.

"People are counting on us. It's nice to have that kind of purpose."

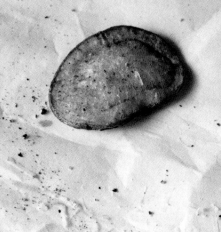

WEISER FAMILY FARMS / **LOS ANGELES**

HOMEMADE CAYENNE-PECORINO POTATO CHIPS

SERVES 6 TO 8 AS A SNACK

6 cups peanut oil, for frying

6 cups cold water

2 tablespoons fine sea salt

1 tablespoon baking soda

2 russet potatoes (1½ to 2 pounds), scrubbed

¼ cup kosher salt

¼ cup freshly grated Pecorino Romano

1 tablespoon freshly ground black pepper

2 teaspoons ground cayenne

1 cup plain Greek yogurt

Homemade chips are an entirely different animal from packaged ones, and are definitely worth the effort.
Make.
A.
Lot.

Fill a large, heavy pot no higher than halfway with oil and heat over medium-high heat until it registers 350°F on a deep-fry thermometer.

Stir together the water, fine sea salt, and baking soda.

Slice the potatoes 1/16 inch thick and toss them into the water mixture for 10 minutes.

In a small bowl, stir together the kosher salt, Pecorino Romano, pepper, and cayenne.

Drain the sliced potatoes and pat dry.

Add the potato slices to the hot oil in batches, and fry until light golden brown, 2 to 3 minutes. Remove with a spider and drain on paper towels, season with the salt-and-cheese mixture while still warm. Serve with plain yogurt in a little bowl for dipping.

BRAISED LEEKS

with Corn and Chipotle Vinaigrette

When properly braised, a leek can be the creamiest and most soul-satisfying member of the lily family. When combined with this poetic corn vinaigrette, we become interplanetary travelers of the sublime.

SERVES 6 TO 8

FOR THE LEEKS

6 leeks

3 tablespoons plus ½ cup extra-virgin olive oil

1½ cups white wine

4 tablespoons (½ stick) unsalted butter (cut into small cubes)

4 sprigs thyme

3 cloves garlic, thinly sliced

1 cup sliced shallots

Kosher salt and freshly ground black pepper

FOR THE VINAIGRETTE

1 cup fresh or frozen corn kernels (4 ears)

1 tablespoon kosher salt, plus more as needed

1 teaspoon Dijon mustard

1 tablespoon chipotle flakes

¼ cup red wine vinegar

Freshly ground black pepper

½ cup extra-virgin olive oil

2 scallions, minced

MAKE THE LEEKS

Trim the roots off the leeks, leaving the root end intact. Trim the tops on an angle, leaving 2 inches of green. Cut the leeks in half lengthwise (the root holds the leeks together while cooking). Clean very well in water to remove any sand or grit.

In a 15-inch sauté pan, heat 3 tablespoons of the olive oil over medium heat. Lay the leeks in the pan, cut side down, without crowding them. Add the wine, butter, thyme, garlic, shallots, and 1½ cups water. Season with a pinch of salt and cracked black pepper. Bring to a boil, then reduce the heat to maintain a simmer. Put a lid on the pan and gently cook for 30 minutes, or until fork-tender.

MAKE THE VINAIGRETTE

Place the corn in a small saucepan with 2 cups of water and 1 tablespoon salt and set over medium heat. Bring to a steamy simmer and cook for 4 minutes, then drain and allow to cool. (You could also put the corn in a glass bowl just covered with water and microwave for 90 seconds.) Combine the corn, mustard, chipotle, and vinegar. Season with salt and pepper and then pour in the olive oil. The vinaigrette should not be creamy and emulsified; it should look broken with rivulets.

Transfer the leeks to a side towel to drain a bit, then place them on a platter. Stir the scallions into the vinaigrette and spoon the vinaigrette over the leeks. Serve warm or at room temperature.

CREAMY KALE GRATIN

This dish is the best of steakhouse-style creamed spinach with a rich mineral backbone that makes it work even better with big steak and red wine. If you want to jack it up a bit, add some bacon to the onion when you are cooking it for the béchamel.

SERVES 6 TO 8

2 tablespoons kosher salt, plus more as needed

6 tablespoons (¾ stick) unsalted butter, plus more for the baking dish

½ cup chopped Spanish or white onion

2 whole cloves

¼ cup all-purpose flour

2 cups whole milk

3 bunches kale (about 1½ pounds), roughly chopped

½ cup plus 2 tablespoons grated Parmigiano-Reggiano

½ teaspoon freshly grated nutmeg

Freshly ground black pepper

Bring 8 quarts water to a boil and add 2 tablespoons salt. Set up an ice bath in a large bowl.

Preheat the oven to 375°F. Butter a 9-inch round gratin dish.

In a heavy-bottomed, medium saucepan, melt the butter over medium heat. Add the onion and cloves and cook until golden brown, about 10 minutes.

Add the flour and stir until light golden brown, about 7 minutes.

Gradually whisk in the milk and cook until the mixture boils and thickens, about 10 minutes.

Reduce the heat to low and simmer, whisking frequently, for 5 minutes more. Remove the cloves.

Add the kale to the boiling water and cook until just wilted and tender, about 2 minutes. Drain the kale and transfer to the ice bath to cool for 5 minutes, then drain well.

Roll up the cooked kale in a kitchen towel or cheesecloth and squeeze out as much liquid as possible.

Finely chop the cooked kale, then add it to the warm sauce. Add ½ cup of the Parmigiano and the nutmeg, season with salt and pepper, and mix well.

Pour the mixture into the buttered gratin dish, top with the remaining 2 tablespoons Parmigiano, and bake for 30 minutes, until bubbly.

ZUCCHINI FRIES

with Tomato Aioli

The crisp exterior afforded by the egg white dip makes these a low-fat, high-texture snack that seems decadent and yet delivers a healthy crunch.

MAKES 24 FRIES

FOR THE AIOLI

2 large egg yolks (reserve the whites for the zucchini fries)

1 clove garlic

Zest and juice of 1 lemon

1 tablespoon tomato paste

2 tablespoons warm water

1 cup extra-virgin olive oil

Kosher salt

FOR THE ZUCCHINI FRIES

Olive oil cooking spray

1 teaspoon dried thyme, crumbled

1 teaspoon dried oregano, crumbled

½ cup all-purpose flour

1 tablespoon kosher salt

1½ cups panko bread crumbs

¾ cup freshly grated Parmigiano-Reggiano

3 large egg whites, whipped to very soft peaks

4 medium zucchini, trimmed

MAKE THE AIOLI

Place the egg yolks, garlic, lemon zest and juice, tomato paste, and water in a blender and blend until smooth. With the motor running, drizzle in the oil until a creamy sauce is formed. Season with salt and set aside.

MAKE THE ZUCCHINI FRIES

Preheat the oven to 475°F. Spray a baking sheet with olive oil cooking spray.

In a pie pan or shallow bowl, mix together the thyme, oregano, flour, and salt. Place the panko and Parmigiano-Reggiano in a separate pie pan or shallow bowl and place the whipped egg whites in a third pie pan or shallow bowl.

Slice each zucchini in half lengthwise and then each half into 3 pieces lengthwise to create steak fry–shaped pieces.

Dredge the zucchini fries in the flour mixture and then dip them into the egg whites. Finally, dredge them in the panko. Place the coated zucchini on the prepared baking sheet and roast, turning once, until crispy, about 12 minutes.

Serve hot, with the aioli on the side.

PANELLE

with Zucchini and Corn Salsa

I love panelle in any form, but perhaps my faves are served in carts in the Vucciria market in Palermo. The addition of corn and zucchini as a salsa would seem superfluous to a true Siciliana, but makes a lot of sense to me.

SERVES 4

FOR THE SALSA

2 tablespoons extra-virgin olive oil

2 ears corn, husked, kernels cut from cobs

1 medium zucchini, cut into ¼-inch dice

4 plum tomatoes, cut into ¼-inch dice, with juices and seeds

½ red onion, cut into ⅛-inch dice

2 jalapeños, stemmed, seeded, and finely chopped

2 tablespoons chopped fresh cilantro

2 tablespoons chopped fresh mint leaves

3 scallions, thinly sliced

Zest and juice of 1 lime

1 teaspoon ground cumin

Kosher salt

FOR THE PANELLE

1 cup chickpea flour

1 teaspoon kosher salt

3 cups cold water

1 bunch fresh flat-leaf parsley, finely chopped (¼ cup), plus more for garnish, if desired

1 quart extra-virgin olive oil, for frying (you may use less than this amount, but have it ready)

MAKE THE CORN SALSA

In a cast-iron skillet, heat the olive oil until smoking. Toss in the corn and the zucchini and do not move it for 2 minutes—be patient. After 2 minutes, shake the pan twice to move the vegetables and continue to cook for 2 minutes more. The corn and zucchini should have a nice char on a couple of sides. Dump the mixture into a medium bowl. Add the rest of the salsa ingredients and mix gently. Set aside.

MAKE THE PANELLE

In a 4- to 6-quart saucepan, dissolve the chickpea flour and salt in the water. Cook over medium-high heat, stirring continuously, until the mixture has the consistency of cream of wheat, about 20 minutes. Stir in the parsley and spread the mixture onto a baking sheet, flattening it to a thickness of about ½ inch, and allow to cool. Using a biscuit or cookie cutter, cut into 2½-inch rounds and refrigerate for 30 minutes.

Heat 2 inches of cooking oil in a high-sided frying pan to 375°F. Fry the chickpea disks, 4 or 5 at a time, until golden brown, 30 to 45 seconds. Carefully remove them from the oil using a spider or a slotted spatula (tongs will tear them), and drain on paper towels.

Serve the panelle hot. Season the salsa with salt and serve on the side, or spoon over the top of each panella, and sprinkle with parsley—or not.

FRIED OKRA
with Gumbo Mustard

Crunchy, salty okra has none of the slime I associate with this gumbo warhorse. The texture is crisp and there is an al dente bite to it, almost like pasta. Be sure to fry the okra at 375°F, and do not crowd the pan, which would drop the temperature.

SERVES 4 TO 6

FOR THE GUMBO MUSTARD

1 cup Creole mustard

2 tablespoons gumbo filé

2 tablespoons Crystal hot sauce

FOR THE FRIED OKRA

1 pound fresh okra

3 large eggs

¼ cup ice water

2 cups semolina

1 tablespoon kosher salt

1 tablespoon lemon pepper

1 teaspoon ground cayenne

Vegetable or canola oil, for frying

Sea salt

MAKE THE GUMBO MUSTARD

In a wide bowl, stir together the mustard, filé, and hot sauce and set aside.

MAKE THE FRIED OKRA

Trim the stem ends off the okra. Cut the pods in half and set aside.

In a large bowl, beat the eggs with the ice water. Set aside.

In a second large bowl, combine the semolina, salt, lemon pepper, and cayenne and set aside.

In a large, heavy pot, heat at least a half an inch of oil until it registers 375°F on a deep-fry thermometer.

While the oil heats, place the okra pieces in the egg mixture and toss to thoroughly and completely coat. Lift out the okra and drain in a colander.

Working in batches of 4 or 5 pods, toss the drained okra into the semolina mixture to coat, then transfer to a baking sheet. Repeat with the remaining okra.

Fry the okra in batches—the pods shouldn't touch—until golden brown and crispy. Use a spider to transfer the cooked okra to a layer of paper towels to drain. Repeat with the remaining okra.

Sprinkle with sea salt and serve hot, with the gumbo mustard on the side for dippin'.

Cleveland

Chef:
MICHAEL SYMON, LOLITA

Farmer:
MAGGIE FITZPATRICK,
REFUGEE RESPONSE AT OHIO CITY FARM

Ingredients:
EGGPLANT, SUMMER SQUASH, OKRA

Maggie Fitzpatrick sits down for dinner at Lolita, Chef Michael Symon's spot in the Tremont neighborhood of Cleveland.

She and her dinner companions order a range of appetizers, including the Eggplant and Feta Dip. More dishes appear. The kitchen wants her to try some things.

First there's a salad of beets cooked in sherry. Then a plate of blistered shishito peppers with lemon zest. That one isn't even on the menu.

Neither are the fried green tomatoes with Fresno chile–Greek yogurt.

Entrées haven't been considered yet, and everyone is stuffed.

Coincidence played no role in the dishes sent to Maggie's table. Michael's executive chef at Lolita, James Mowcomber, sent her the ingredients she delivered to the restaurant this week. The eggplant. The beets. The shishitos and tomatoes. All things Maggie and her crew grew.

"Thanks for treating my vegetables so well!" she tells James as she leaves.

Maggie is the farm manager for Refugee Response, an organization that helps refugees acclimate to the United States by, among other things, developing agricultural skills they can use to find work.

Maggie has experience farming in another country herself. After she earned her master's degree in biology at Michigan State, she joined a program that took her from farm to farm in Ireland. For a year, she and a friend worked at farms along the country's west coast. In Cork, Mayo, Clare, and Donegal, she grew vegetables and tended livestock.

Afterward, she returned to her hometown of Cleveland intent on applying her degree and the things she learned in her travels. She took a desk job with Ohio City Farm, which manages a five-and-a-half-acre plot overlooking the Cuyahoga River and has a postcard view of the Cleveland skyline.

It didn't take long before she wanted to get her hands dirty.

Refugee Response, one of the groups farming Ohio City's land, needed a new manager. The organization helps people who have been admitted to the country from distressed situations—from places such as Liberia, Burma, and Nepal—adjust to a new culture. The focus is on tutoring students, but there's also an agriculture program. Many refugees have an agrarian skill set, and Refugee Response empowers them by helping them apply skills they know in a country they don't.

Just like Maggie did in Ireland.

When the farm opened in 2010, organizers walked around the neighborhood with baskets of produce to show chefs what was growing right around the corner. Restaurants touting sustainability had to get on board with ingredients that could be delivered by foot.

The farm started growing things the restaurants wanted, but it got interesting when the trainees started suggesting they grow things that reminded them of their homelands. They talked Maggie into growing crops like red okra, long beans, and sweet potatoes. Things the restaurants didn't order…until they heard they were available. Then they wanted all they could get.

Part of Maggie's job is to help make sure nothing gets lost in translation for the trainees.

So when Burmese women tell Maggie that they use the leaves of squash plants to flavor soup, she patiently asks if they mean they use the squash itself.

No, they say, the leaves.

Maggie had never heard of using the squash leaves for anything, so she asked if they meant they use the flowers.

Nope. The leaves.

Maggie didn't want to let this slip as a miscommunication. So she and the women went out to the rows of squash, and she asked them to show her which part of the plant they use in the soup.

They pointed to the leaves. They were surprised at how much of the plant Americans throw away.

It was a teaching moment. You just don't always know who's going to do the learning.

Refugee Response was inspired by a vacation its founders, David Wallis and Paul Neundorfer, took to Thailand. They went for a couple of weeks, but even before they got home, they were planning their return to the Southeast Asian country.

David went back immediately and spent the next five years teaching English at a university there. One of his students was Thomas Kate, who had spent years in a refugee camp on the border with Burma. In David's class, Thomas wrote an essay about how he had been abducted by soldiers when he was a child. The harrowing

tale made David and Paul want to learn more, to help more.

When David returned to Cleveland, he and Paul looked into what happens to refugees who make it to the United States. They learned refugees get just a couple of months of support before they're on their own. David and Paul wanted to help extend the process.

They learned about the Ohio City land, where a housing project had been scuttled because the property's slope left it unstable. Too unstable for a major construction project, maybe, but perfect to give people new to the country some footing.

As David and Paul were starting Refugee Response, they learned Thomas and his family had immigrated to New York and that their transition had been rough. So they drove to New York and picked them up.

Thomas is now the organization's programs coordinator. He helps identify candidates for the farming program. He helps them with paperwork. He sits with them at the DMV when they need new identification.

But his favorite job is on the farm.

He grew rice in Thailand, but he likes the diversity of crops here. He likes growing squash. He likes the leaves. In soup, sure, he says, but they're good just stir-fried with some garlic, too.

As Maggie makes her rounds at the farm, she comes to the sweet potato patch where Daniel, who came from Liberia, is dutifully weeding. Weeds here never have a chance.

Maggie asks Daniel if he likes sweet potatoes. He says he does, and that he especially likes making a soup from the leaves.

More soup from leaves!

In an increasingly excited tone, he explains that the leaves give you more blood. He emphasizes the point by beating his chest.

You mean that it improves circulation? Maggie asks.

"More blood!" He is insistent, and beats his chest harder.

She acknowledges that she understands and tells him he should make the soup because she'd like to taste it. She walks away, on to her next task.

Who knows? Maybe sweet potato leaves give you more blood.

OKRA PICKLES

These crunchy, sweet, and vinegary pickles make the party, and are perfect as a hostess gift when we are occasionally invited to someone else's house for dinner. As a host, I love getting home-made stuff, much more than a bottle of wine.

MAKES 2 QUARTS

2 pounds large fresh okra, stems trimmed to ¼ inch

4 small dried chipotle peppers

4 cloves garlic, halved

1 tablespoon fennel seeds

1 tablespoon coriander seeds

1 teaspoon whole black peppercorns

3 cups apple cider vinegar

½ cup sugar

3 tablespoons kosher salt

3 cups water

Divide the okra, chipotle, and garlic among four sterilized 1-pint canning jars. Divide the fennel seeds, coriander seeds, and peppercorns evenly among the jars.

In a medium saucepan, combine the vinegar, sugar, salt, and water and bring to a boil over high heat, stirring to dissolve the sugar and salt. Pour the brine over the okra, leaving ½ inch of headspace at the top of each jar. Close the jars with sterilized lids and rings.

To process, boil the jars at 212°F for 10 minutes (see the canning process for tomatoes on page 272). Cool to room temperature and let pickle for a week before opening, or store in a cool, dark place for up to 1 year. Refrigerate after opening.

TEMPURA GREEN BEANS

with Tomato Seed Aioli

Vegetarian appetizers are the best way to get the meat-and-potato folks involved in the world of green glory. These crisp heroes make it even easier.

SERVES 4

FOR THE TOMATO SEED AIOLI

2 egg yolks

Zest and juice of 1 lemon

2 cloves garlic, finely minced

1 heirloom tomato

½ cup extra-virgin olive oil

Kosher salt and freshly ground
    black pepper

FOR THE GREEN BEANS

4 cups peanut oil, for frying

Zest of 1 lemon

1½ cups cake flour

½ teaspoon baking soda

2 teaspoons kosher salt

1 (12-ounce) bottle or can of lager
    beer, cold

2 egg yolks

1 pound thin green beans or
    haricots verts, trimmed

Fine salt

MAKE THE AIOLI

In a blender, combine the egg yolks, lemon zest, lemon juice, and garlic and blend until smooth. Cut the tomato in half crosswise and squeeze the juices and seeds into the blender, squeezing hard to get them all. With the blender running on low, drizzle in the olive oil in a thin stream until a thick emulsion is formed. Pour into a dipping bowl, season with salt and pepper, and set aside.

MAKE THE GREEN BEANS

Heat 3 inches of oil in a deep saucepan until it registers 365°F on a deep-fry thermometer. Line a plate with paper towels.

Place the lemon zest in a medium bowl and set it over a larger bowl of ice. Add the cake flour, baking soda, and kosher salt to the bowl with the zest. Stir together the beer and egg yolks in a small cup. Whisk the egg mixture into the flour mixture until barely combined—there will still be a few lumps, but do not worry.

Dredge the beans in the tempura batter and drop them, one by one, into the hot oil. Fry until light golden brown and crisp. Do not overcrowd the pan. There should never be more than half the surface of the oil covered with beans. Using a spider, transfer the fried beans to the paper towel–lined plate and season immediately with fine salt, then serve with a dipping bowl of the aioli on the side.

OVEN-DRIED TOMATOES / CANNED TOMATOES

If you have your own tomato plants, you know that the end of the season comes fast and voluminously, and you need to do something to use the sweet harvest. These are my two favorite ways to extend my summer bounty into the cool fall and cold winter. It's also a great family activity, so start an annual tradition and bring your family into the production process.

OVEN-DRIED TOMATOES

MAKES 6 CUPS

4 pounds ripe plum tomatoes

3 tablespoons kosher salt

3 tablespoons sugar

Leaves from 2 bunches fresh thyme

6 cloves garlic, grated on a
    Microplane

1 cup extra-virgin olive oil

Preheat the oven to 200°F.

Slice the tomatoes in half lengthwise and place them in a large bowl. Add the salt, sugar, thyme, garlic, and oil and toss to coat well. Place cut side up on baking sheets, then bake slowly for 12 hours. (Putting the tomatoes in the oven right before you go to bed and removing them in the morning works well.) Let cool and refrigerate for later use. If you pack them in sterile glass jars and cover them completely with more extra-virgin olive oil, they can be stored in the refrigerator for up to 12 weeks.

Continued on page 272.

CANNED TOMATOES

Bring a pot of water to a simmer for the jar lids. Bring a saucepan of water to a boil for the tomatoes. Set up an ice bath. Fill a water bath canner or stockpot with water and heat it to just below boiling.

Wash the jars in hot soapy water and rinse. Check the rims for nicks or cracks. If you feel a nick in the rim, do not use the jar. It will never be able to form a vacuum seal.

Wash the lids and rings in hot soapy water and rinse. Place them in the pan of simmering water.

Fill the sink with hot water and leave the jars submerged in the water. Add more hot water from time to time to make sure the jars stay nice and hot.

Wash the tomatoes well and drain. Make an X with a paring knife at the point and also remove the stem and core. Dip the tomatoes into the saucepan of boiling water for 30 to 60 seconds, or until the skins split. Then dip into the ice water. Peel off the skins and set the tomatoes in a large bowl until you finish them all.

Place 2 tablespoons of the lemon juice in each jar. Using the funnel, pack as many tomatoes into each jar as you can. I usually pack them in layers, stem side down. Cut the tomatoes in half to fit as many as you can in the jars, leaving about 1 inch of headspace at the top. Add 1 tablespoon of salt to the top of the tomatoes, then add 2 basil leaves, sliding them a bit down the side of the jar.

Add hot water to cover, leaving ½ inch of headspace at the top.

Wipe the whole jar with a clean cloth to remove any spillage.

Place a lid on the jar, then tighten the ring over it to create an airtight seal.

Place the jars in the water bath canner in hot, but not boiling, water. Make sure the water covers them by 1 to 2 inches. If you need more water, heat it in a kettle and pour it over. If you have too much water, use a ladle to scoop it out and pour it into another container. Cover the pot and bring to a boil. Once the water returns to boiling, start timing. Process the jars for 45 minutes, always at a boil.

Using tongs, remove the jars from the hot water and place them on a dry kitchen towel with plenty of space around them. Allow to cool for several hours. Notice that the lids start to shrink and create a vacuum seal. These jars can be stored for many months in a dark cool place.

MAKES 6 QUARTS

15 pounds very ripe whole Roma tomatoes or other low-moisture tomatoes (you can certainly use juicier heirloom varieties, but they won't hold their shape as well)

¾ cup bottled lemon juice

6 tablespoons kosher salt

12 fresh basil leaves

YOU WILL NEED

6 (1-quart) wide-mouth jars with sealable lids and rings

Water bath canner (or stockpot) and canning rack

Jar-lifter tongs

Wide-mouth funnel

SWEET AND HOT TOMATO JAM

It takes a little time to make, but this is a condiment I will put on anything from Parmigiano-Reggiano, to an omelet, to fried chicken. I must warn you about its addictive properties…So beware, and stock up.

MAKES 2 QUARTS

4 pounds ripe tomatoes

2 tablespoons honey

Zest and juice of 1 lemon

2 serrano chiles, sliced paper thin

1 tablespoon kosher salt

2 tablespoons sugar

1 teaspoon red pepper flakes

Bring 4 quarts water to a boil. Set up an ice bath near the stovetop.

Using a paring knife, score the tomatoes with an X at the point end and drop the tomatoes into the boiling water for 30 seconds, then transfer to the ice bath. Peel the tomatoes then chop them and place in a medium saucepan with the honey, lemon zest, lemon juice, chiles, salt, sugar, and red pepper flakes. Stir and bring to a simmer. Clip a candy thermometer to the pan and cook, stirring occasionally, until the mixture registers 220°F (it should have a thick, syrupy consistency), 1½ to 2 hours.

Put the jam in a jar or use immediately. It will keep covered tightly in the fridge for up to 2 weeks.

Eight:
DESSERTS

MY CARROT, HAZELNUT, AND GINGER CAKE

MAKES ONE 9-BY-13-INCH RECTANGULAR OR 8-INCH ROUND CAKE

FOR THE CAKE

Butter and flour, for the pan

4 large eggs

1 cup Hellman's olive oil mayonnaise

1 cup granulated sugar

1 cup light brown sugar, packed

1 tablespoon pure vanilla extract

2 cups all-purpose flour

2 teaspoons baking soda

2 teaspoons baking powder

1 teaspoon kosher salt

¼ cup grated fresh peeled ginger

2 teaspoons ground cinnamon

2½ cups grated carrots (from about 1 pound whole carrots)

¾ cup roughly chopped hazelnuts

FOR THE FROSTING

8 tablespoons (1 stick) unsalted butter, softened

8 ounces cream cheese, softened

3 cups confectioners' sugar

¼ cup molasses

I am not a big fan of sticky or cloying cakes, but I always love both beet-driven red velvet cake and this carrot cake, for their moist but firm texture and their haunting vegetal sweetness, which reminds me more of great wine than crazy desserts. The mayonnaise in the cake makes it especially moist, and I really like the molasses in the frosting—it seems odd but is crazy good.

MAKE THE CAKE

Preheat the oven to 350°F. Grease and flour a 9-by-13-inch pan or an 8-inch springform pan.

In a large bowl, beat together the eggs, mayonnaise, granulated sugar, brown sugar, and vanilla. Mix in the flour, baking soda, baking powder, salt, ginger, and cinnamon. Stir in the carrots. Fold in the hazelnuts and pour the batter into the prepared pan.

Bake for 40 to 50 minutes, until a toothpick inserted into the center of the cake comes out clean. Let cool in the pan for 10 minutes, then turn out onto a wire rack and cool completely.

MAKE THE FROSTING

In a medium bowl, combine the butter, cream cheese, confectioners' sugar, and molasses. Beat until the mixture is smooth and creamy, then slather it on the cooled cake.

PEACH CLAFOUTIS

SERVES 12

Butter, for the pan

1¼ cups whole milk

⅔ cup granulated sugar

3 large eggs

1 tablespoon pure vanilla extract

1 teaspoon ground cardamom

⅛ teaspoon kosher salt

½ cup almond flour

3 ripe peaches, pitted and sliced

Confectioners' sugar, for dusting

This is as much an almond pancake as it is a fancy dessert and may be the single-best example of "bang for your buck" in the impress-your-friends department. Originally made of cherries with pits in the Limousin region of south-central France, I adapted it to use peaches, but you can sub any stone fruit in season where you are.

Preheat the oven to 350°F. Lightly butter a 9-by-13-inch heatproof baking dish or pan.

In a blender, blend the milk, ⅓ cup of the granulated sugar, the eggs, vanilla, cardamom, salt, and almond flour. Pour a ¼-inch layer of the batter into the prepared baking dish. Place in the oven and bake until a film of batter sets in the pan, 2 to 3 minutes.

Remove from the oven and spread the peaches over the batter. Sprinkle the remaining ⅓ cup granulated sugar evenly over the top. Pour the remaining batter over the peaches.

Bake for 45 minutes to 1 hour. The clafoutis is done when puffed and brown and a knife plunged into the center comes out clean.

Dust with confectioners' sugar and serve warm.

PEACHES IN RED WINE SYRUP

SERVES 4

2 cups sugar

2 cups dry red wine (my fave is zinfandel)

1 whole clove

4 peaches

Serving fruit with red wine is a big tradition in Puglia, where they often chill the raisiny red local wines and simply pour them over sliced fresh peaches. I have spiced up the wine and also sweetened it a bit to create a more syrupy liquid. It also works well with cherries. There will be some extra sauce: I use it on pancakes or crepes in the morning.

In a medium saucepan, combine the sugar, red wine, and clove, bring to a simmer, and simmer until reduced by half, about 30 minutes. Let cool and remove the clove. (The syrup can be made ahead and refrigerated for up to 1 week.)

Peel, pit, and slice the peaches and divide evenly among four footed bowls. Pour one-quarter of the syrup over each portion and serve.

PEACH SHORTCAKE

These yogurt biscuits are spectacular warm, or made the day before and toasted in butter in a sauté pan. Go out and find some local peaches and celebrate the end of summer in a way that befits the queen of stone fruit.

MAKES 12 BISCUITS

FOR THE BUTTER AND YOGURT BISCUITS

2 cups all-purpose flour, plus more for dusting

1 tablespoon kosher salt

3 teaspoons baking powder

2 teaspoons baking soda

12 tablespoons (1½ sticks) unsalted butter, cold, cut into ¼-inch pieces

1 cup plain Greek yogurt

FOR THE WHIPPED CREAM

2 pints whipping cream

¼ cup honey

1 teaspoon pure vanilla extract

TO ASSEMBLE

8 peaches

Zest and juice of 1 orange

½ teaspoon kosher salt

2 tablespoons honey

MAKE THE BUTTER AND YOGURT BISCUITS

Preheat the oven to 450°F. Line a baking sheet with parchment paper.

Place the flour, salt, baking powder, and baking soda in a food processor and pulse until combined. Add the butter and pulse a few more times, until the butter is thoroughly cut into the flour mixture.

Add the yogurt and pulse the mixture a couple of times to stir it in, just until the mixture comes together. Turn the dough out onto a floured counter and knead it 6 times only. The dough should be a little tacky.

Press the dough to a 1-inch thickness and cut it into rounds using a floured biscuit cutter, pressing straight down without twisting.

Place the biscuits on the parchment paper–lined baking sheet. Reshape the dough scraps and cut more biscuits. Bake for 7 to 10 minutes, until light golden brown.

MAKE THE WHIPPED CREAM

Put a large bowl into the freezer to chill.

When you are ready to whip the cream, take the bowl out of the freezer and pour in the cream. Whip to soft peaks, then gently stir in the honey and vanilla.

ASSEMBLE THE SHORTCAKE

Peel, pit, and slice the peaches. Toss them in a bowl with the orange zest, orange juice, salt, and honey and mix gently.

When the biscuits are done, take them out of the oven and cut them in half. Top the biscuits with the dressed peaches and whipped cream.

ALMOND AND HONEY BRITTLE

MAKES 1 POUND

¼ cup almond oil

4 cups sliced blanched almonds

2 cups sugar

1 cup honey

¼ cup water

Crunchy, sharp, and dangerously addictive.

Preheat the oven to 400°F. Grease a baking sheet with the almond oil.

Place the almonds on a separate baking sheet and toast them in the oven until light golden brown, about 5 minutes. Set aside.

In a medium, very heavy-bottomed saucepan, combine the sugar, honey, and water and cook over medium-high heat until the sugar liquefies, then turns light golden brown, 15 to 20 minutes. It should register 310°F on a candy thermometer; this is referred to as the "hard-crack" stage. Do not stir, but brush the sugar crystals off the inside of the pan with a wet pastry brush as necessary. Once the sugar begins to brown (to the color of a football), remove the pan from the heat (watch very carefully, as the sugar can burn quickly).

Once the caramel is off the heat, add the almonds to the pot and stir quickly to incorporate. Turn the caramel mixture out onto the prepared baking sheet, spreading it quickly to an even thickness. Let the brittle cool completely, then break it into pieces or cut into shapes with a serrated knife.

Las Vegas

Chef:
DOUG TAYLOR, B&B LAS VEGAS

Farmer:
JON CHODACKI, UNCE ORCHARD

Ingredients:
STONE FRUIT, ALMONDS, FIGS

Las Vegas isn't the first place you think of for an al fresco dinner, but when a charity set a 150-seat dining table in the orchard of the University of Nevada, Reno, Cooperative Extension in North

Las Vegas, every seat was full.

Jon Chodacki, the manager of the orchard, was impressed by the spread. Chefs from the B&B restaurants at the Venetian and Palazzo resorts cooked a menu inspired by crops from the region. Doug Taylor, B&B's executive pastry chef, was in charge of dessert. He took peaches grown on the grounds, split them in half, and grilled them on grates that had just cooked pork loins.

The peaches slow-roasted over dying embers, resulting in a super-soft, super-sweet, super-simple dessert.

Jon was surprised by the elemental presentation. The other dishes were quite elaborate. Why didn't his ingredient get more adornment?

Because, Doug told him, they didn't need it. They were perfect.

"That was probably the best compliment I've ever gotten."

Organizers of an arborist convention wanted Jon to speak at their event. He eluded their calls. They kept calling. Finally he asked, "Why is it so important that I speak?"

Because you're the state's leading authority on fruit trees, they told him.

That was how he found out.

If you look around his modest 2.2-acre orchard, it's easy to see how he earned that reputation. He's growing about five hundred fruit trees in more than one hundred fifty varieties…in the middle of the desert.

In Las Vegas, lush landscaping gives a green base to the city's canopy of neon. But it's a mirage. To grow anything in the desert, you have to beat the desert.

Jon's job isn't to grow fruit—it's to figure out how *other people* can. Very few of his trees are exactly the same. He tests different varieties with different root stocks using different pruning methods in different combinations, all to determine what can be tricked into succeeding here.

People love dwarf fruit trees because the fruit is easy to harvest. Have fun, Jon says, because they won't thrive. They don't produce the foliage they need to protect the fruit.

He likes almonds and figs. They'll grow fifty feet tall and can provide a windbreak to protect other crops.

People ask him how to grow apples and pears. Jon tried, but it takes a lot of work to get those to thrive in the desert. Try a pomegranate tree, he says. They go crazy.

After living in San Francisco and Hawaii, Doug struggled to find a local food scene in Vegas. When he found the orchard, he spent an entire day under a tree eating fruit.

He became dedicated to getting local fruit on his menu, which meant supporting and developing farmers. He got good enough at it that the extension service hired him to help other restaurants do it, too. If that sounds like helping the competition, it's not. Increasing the demand for local food would increase the number of farmers. Doug said they couldn't afford to be selfish.

He and Jon found farmers from outlying areas to bring food into the city. Jon cultivated farmers closer to home. Janet Knight and Marilyn Yamamoto earned master gardener status through the extension service and took what they learned from Jon and his predecessor, Bob Morris, to start small, residential farms. Rodney Mehring tends the beehives at the orchard for Jon. He started a farm where he grows greens for restaurants in the city.

Doug and Jon started Bet on the Farm, the first producer-to-chef farmers' market in the city. Chefs came and met the farmers. It became so popular, other markets started popping up around the city.

Competition?

That was the plan. There's no reason to be selfish.

A walk through the orchard with Jon is a chance for a tasting tour.

The first stop is a tree labeled "Flavor Supreme." It's a pluot tree, a cross between a plum and an apricot. It's next to trees called "Flavor Queen" and "Flavor King." Jon wants to show us the pluot to tell us we aren't ready for it yet. It would ruin the rest of the fruit for us. He picks a Queen and hands out slices, explaining how the sweetness and tartness hit different parts of the palate. Next is a King. He says the sweet and tart levels are different, as is the way you taste them. You can tell what he means, but you might never have noticed the differences on your own.

He's a sommelier of stone fruit.

The tour continues with peaches. Jon doesn't like how thick the skin is, but says that just happens in the desert. It hardly seems like a problem, but we learn what causes it and that there's nothing we can do about it.

We snake through trees that aren't bearing right now. Almonds and pistachios. Persimmons and pomegranate. Apples and pears (never stop trying!). We carefully make our way past the beehives.

We're deemed ready for Flavor Supremes. Frankly, the hype makes it hard to imagine being as impressed as we're expected to be.

One bite, and the sweetness overwhelms any other sensory data.

Jon explains Brix, more wine vernacular. It's a measure of sugar content, the science of sweet. He says that this pluot is about 29 Brix, but he has had them as high as 38. Doug says

that when he makes a sorbet, he aims for 22 to 25 Brix. Any more and it won't freeze correctly. To use these in a sorbet, he'd have to tone down the sweetness.

The tour is over, and the tourists are on a sugar high.

Jon grows grapes at the orchard, and students make a few jugs of wine, strictly for scientific purposes. Jon's interest is limited. He doesn't drink wine.

But Nevada's governor got Jon's undivided attention when he asked Jon to see if hops would grow in Las Vegas.

Jon turned a hoop house in the orchard into a hop house, growing several varieties in different conditions to see what works. The early results look good, but trial and error can take years.

If there's a way, Jon will figure it out. That's his job.

FIG TART
with Almond Crust

SERVES 12

FOR THE CRUST

Butter, for the tart pan

½ cup blanched almonds, lightly toasted

2 teaspoons aniseeds

1 cup all-purpose flour, plus more as needed

6 tablespoons (¾ stick) unsalted butter, very cold, cut into small cubes

½ cup confectioners' sugar

1 teaspoon fine sea salt

1 large egg, lightly beaten with 1 tablespoon cold water

FOR THE CUSTARD

1½ cups heavy cream

4 fresh sage leaves

1 teaspoon aniseeds, crushed

1 large egg, lightly beaten

1 tablespoon confectioners' sugar

TO ASSEMBLE

12 ripe black or green figs

24 whole blanched almonds, lightly toasted

2 tablespoons dark brown sugar

Figs are a tough sell to many of my pals, until they try this tart where the sweet, rich fruit is a million miles away from the sugary Fig Newton. The anise in the crust and the custard makes this a little exotic, a perfect match for a rich red wine like amarone as a showstopping beverage pairing.

MAKE THE CRUST

Preheat the oven to 400°F. Butter a 10-inch tart pan.

In the bowl of a food processor, pulse the almonds with the aniseeds, breaking them into coarse crumbs. Add the flour, butter, confectioners' sugar, and salt and pulse 10 to 12 times to create coarse crumbs. Add the egg and pulse 8 to 10 times, just until the pastry begins to come together.

Turn the mixture out onto a lightly floured work surface and form it into a ball. Flatten the ball with a floured rolling pin, and press the dough into the bottom and sides of the prepared tart pan. Cover with plastic wrap and place in the freezer for 30 minutes.

Prick the surface of the pastry all over with a fork. Bake the crust for 12 to 14 minutes until it is firm and pale golden brown, then remove from the oven and let cool.

Reduce the oven temperature to 375°F.

MAKE THE CUSTARD

In a medium saucepan, combine the cream, sage, and aniseeds and bring to a simmer over medium-high heat. Reduce the heat to medium-low and cook until reduced by one-third. Remove the pan from the heat and let cool to room temperature. Pour the cream through a strainer into a bowl to remove the sage and anise; discard the solids left in the strainer. Add the egg and confectioners' sugar to the cream, blending carefully.

ASSEMBLE THE TART

Halve the figs lengthwise and stuff each fig half with an almond. Lay the stuffed figs, cut side up, in the pastry shell.

Pour the custard over and around the figs. Dust the top with the brown sugar and bake the tart for 35 minutes, or until the custard is set. Remove from the oven and let cool for 10 minutes. Carefully remove the tart from the pan and let the tart cool for 20 minutes more before serving.

RASPBERRY-GRAPEFRUIT POPSICLES

Fresh local raspberries sing in a different key with pink grapefruit juice. Come along and join the chorus. You will need conical molds or paper cups and popsicle sticks for this.

MAKES 8 POPSICLES

2 cups fresh raspberries

1½ cups pink grapefruit juice

3 tablespoons crème de cassis

In a blender, puree 1½ cups of the raspberries, the grapefruit juice, and the crème de cassis until smooth.

Divide the puree among the cone molds or paper cups. Divide the remaining raspberries among the molds. Cover and freeze until firm, about an hour. Stick popsicle sticks into the center of each and freeze for 2 hours more, or until solid.

RASPBERRY-RICOTTA PANCAKES

These are cloudlike pancakes that will hover around your breakfast table like good ideas and Bach cello concertos. Lie down on your back, relax, and float downstream…

MAKES 10 TO 12 PANCAKES

¾ cup cake flour

2 tablespoons sugar

1 teaspoon kosher salt

Zest of 1 lemon

2 cups fresh ricotta

1½ cups raspberries

6 large eggs, separated

Butter, for the griddle

Grade A maple syrup, for serving

Preheat the oven to 200°F. Heat a nonstick griddle or sauté pan over medium-high heat.

Whisk together the flour, sugar, salt, lemon zest, ricotta, 1 cup of the raspberries, and the egg yolks in a large bowl until smooth and well combined.

Beat the egg whites in a separate bowl until stiff. Gently fold the egg whites into the ricotta mixture.

Melt a small pat of butter on the griddle. Working in batches, ladle ¼ cup of the pancake batter onto the hot griddle and cook for about 2 minutes, until bubbles form nicely on the raw top, then flip and cook until just cooked through, about 2 minutes more. The pancakes will puff up, but then come back down as they rest. Transfer the cooked pancakes to an ovenproof platter and keep warm in the oven while you make the rest of the pancakes.

Serve with maple syrup and the remaining raspberries.

STRAWBERRY SOUP

with Balsamic–Black Pepper Peaches

SERVES 6

2 quarts fresh strawberries, rinsed and hulled

1 cup plain Greek yogurt

¼ cup grapefruit juice

2 tablespoons agave nectar

1 teaspoon ground cardamom

4 tablespoons extra-virgin olive oil

Pinch of kosher salt

2 ripe peaches

4 tablespoons aceto Villa Manodori or best available balsamic vinegar

1 teaspoon freshly cracked black pepper

This is a Proustian dessert for me, taking me back to the childhood joy of the Good Humor truck bells jangling, eating Creamsicles—a similar combination of cream and sour fruit—with the neighborhood kids…creamy texture and bright acidity all in one bite.

Place the strawberries, yogurt, grapefruit juice, agave, cardamom, olive oil, and the salt in a food processor and process until smooth, stopping to scrape down the sides as needed. Cover and chill for 2 hours.

Peel and slice the peaches into 18 thin slices. Place them in a bowl and toss with 2 tablespoons of the balsamic vinegar and pepper. Set aside until ready to serve.

To serve, ladle the soup into shallow bowls, arrange 3 prepared peach slices in the center, and drizzle with the remaining 2 tablespoons of balsamic vinegar.

STRAWBERRY-MASCARPONE OLIVE OIL CAKE

I am not a big frosting fan, but this double-barreled combo of a mascarpone filling and a whipped cream frosting is right in my wheelhouse. The olive oil cake is yummy enough to stand on its own, if you prefer to serve it with just berries and whipped cream.

SERVES 8 TO 10

FOR THE STRAWBERRIES

2 pints strawberries, rinsed and hulled (about 4 cups)

2 tablespoons agave nectar

Zest and juice of 1 lime

FOR THE CAKE

Butter, for the pan

2 cups cake flour, plus more for the pan

2 teaspoons baking powder

1 teaspoon kosher salt

½ cup extra-virgin olive oil

¼ cup whole milk

1 tablespoon pure vanilla extract

6 large eggs, separated

1½ cups sugar

FOR THE FROSTING

1 tablespoon pure vanilla extract

6 tablespoons sugar

1½ cups heavy cream

FOR THE FILLING

1 cup mascarpone cheese

½ cup heavy cream

1 teaspoon Grand Marnier or orange extract

MAKE THE STRAWBERRIES

Combine the strawberries, agave, lime zest, and lime juice in a medium nonreactive bowl and toss to thoroughly coat the strawberries. Let stand for 20 minutes. Separate the juices from the fruit; refrigerate the fruit and leave the juices in the bowl on the counter.

MAKE THE CAKE

Position a rack in the upper third of the oven and preheat to 350°F. Butter and flour two 8-inch cake pans.

Sift together the flour, baking powder, and salt in a bowl; set aside.

In the bowl of a stand mixer fitted with the whip attachment, combine the olive oil, milk, vanilla, egg yolks, and 1¼ cups of the sugar. Mix on high speed until the mixture is airy and light in color, 5 to 7 minutes. Turn off the mixer and scrape down the sides of the bowl; add the dry ingredients and replace the whip with the paddle attachment. Mix on medium speed until smooth, about 1 minute more.

In the clean bowl of a stand mixer fitted with a clean whip attachment, whip the egg whites to medium peaks. Add the remaining ¼ cup sugar and continue whipping until stiff peaks form, about 1 minute more. Stir one-quarter of the egg whites into the cake batter until evenly incorporated; gently fold in the remaining egg whites until just combined.

Divide the batter between the prepared cake pans and bake for about 45 minutes, or until a toothpick inserted into the center of each cake comes out clean. Remove the cakes from the oven and let cool for 15 minutes. Run a knife around the edges of each, and turn them out onto wire racks to cool completely, at least 30 minutes.

Continued on page 302.

MAKE THE FROSTING

Place the bowl of a stand mixer and the whip attachment in the freezer to chill for 10 minutes.

Combine the vanilla, sugar, and heavy cream in the chilled bowl and whip at medium speed until medium peaks form, about 2 minutes.

Cover and refrigerate until well chilled, at least 1 hour.

MAKE THE FILLING

In the clean bowl of a stand mixer fitted with a clean whip attachment, combine the mascarpone, heavy cream, and Grand Marnier and whip until firm peaks form, about 2 minutes. Cover and refrigerate until ready to use.

ASSEMBLE THE CAKE

Using a serrated knife, trim the tops of the cakes as necessary so they are level. Place the cake rounds on a clean, dry surface and brush half of the reserved strawberry liquid on the cut side of the first cake round; repeat on the cut side of the second cake round.

Check the filling and frosting to be sure they are very stiff; if not, re-whip until stiff. Evenly spread one-quarter of the mascarpone filling over the cut side of the bottom cake layer. Arrange the strawberries standing upright, stem end down, over the mascarpone layer and trim as necessary to create an even layer. Pour the remaining filling over the strawberries and fill in any empty spots.

Place the second cake layer over the strawberry layer, cut side down, pressing gently to secure it. Using a thin spatula, spread the frosting in a thin layer over the top and sides of the cake. Chill for at least 15 minutes or up to overnight before serving.

TART CHERRY CRUMB PIE

with Bacon Crust

I am not sure I invented the bacon crust, but man, oh, man, I sure love it. Tart cherries are an entirely different game in the world of cherry pies, and once you have them encased in bacon crust, you will never go back.

MAKES ONE 9-INCH DEEP-DISH PIE OR ONE 11-INCH TART

FOR THE BACON CRUST

1½ cups all-purpose flour

1 teaspoon kosher salt

½ cup plus 1 tablespoon well-chilled bacon, cut into ⅛-inch pieces

5 ounces unsalted butter

⅓ cup ice water

FOR THE CHERRY FILLING

5 cups fresh tart cherries, pitted

1 cup sugar

2½ tablespoons cornstarch

Pinch of kosher salt

Zest and juice of 1 lemon

1 teaspoon pure vanilla extract

FOR THE ALMOND CRUMB TOPPING

¾ cup all-purpose flour

½ cup sugar

⅓ cup finely chopped almonds

¼ teaspoon kosher salt

5 tablespoons unsalted butter, melted

Heavy cream, for serving (optional)

MAKE THE PIE CRUST

Combine the flour and salt in a food processor and process briefly to combine. Add the bacon and butter and pulse until the mixture resembles big bread crumbs.

Sprinkle half of the water over the mixture and pulse 5 or 6 times, pulling the mixture up from the bottom of the bowl. Sprinkle on the remaining water and pulse again 5 or 6 times, briefly, just until the dough pulls together into a ball.

Put the dough on a large flour-dusted piece of waxed paper and flatten it into a disk about 1 inch thick. Wrap tightly in plastic wrap and chill for 1 hour.

MAKE THE FILLING

Combine the cherries and ½ cup of the sugar in a large bowl. Set aside for 10 minutes to macerate. Mix the remaining ½ cup sugar, the cornstarch, and the salt in a small bowl and stir the mixture into the cherries. Stir in the lemon zest, lemon juice, and vanilla and set aside.

MAKE THE ALMOND CRUMB TOPPING

Combine the flour, sugar, almonds, and salt in a food processor and pulse 7 times to blend well. With the motor running, drizzle in the melted butter—this should take 8 pulses, max. The topping should look like sandy gravel, not dough. Set aside.

Continued on page 304.

ASSEMBLE THE PIE

Preheat the oven to 350°F.

Lightly flour a 2-foot piece of waxed paper. Place the chilled pastry in the center of the paper, dust it lightly with flour, then roll it into a 12-inch circle. Turn it out over an 11-inch tart pan, center it, and peel off the paper. Tuck the pastry into the pan, pressing it into the fluted rim without stretching it. Trim the overhang so the pastry is flush with the top of the rim. Place in the freezer for 10 minutes.

Remove the crust from the freezer and pour in the cherry filling, then sprinkle with the almond crumb topping, and "rake" it evenly over the pie.

Place the tart on a parchment-paper lined baking sheet and put it in the oven. Bake it for 1 hour, until bubbling all over.

Remove from the oven and transfer to a wire rack and let cool for at least 2 hours before serving, or you will be having soup with a crumble crust.

Slice and serve with softly whipped unsweetened cream, if desired.

Suttons Bay

Chef:
CAMMIE BUEHLER, EPICURE CATERING

Farmer:
JIM BARDENHAGEN AND GINGER
BARDENHAGEN, BARDENHAGEN FARMS

Ingredients:
CHERRIES, APPLES

In 1978, Vernon Bardenhagen was getting ready to retire. He was the fourth-generation Bardenhagen to farm the land in Suttons Bay, Michigan, that his family homesteaded around

the end of the Civil War. In his more than three decades of running the farm, he grew the potatoes and strawberries the area was known for, and added cherry trees to the land.

His son Jim had left Suttons Bay after high school to study at Michigan State. Then he took a job that sent him and his young family east. Even then, every summer vacation included a return to Suttons Bay to help with the cherry harvest.

He was living in Charleston, West Virginia, when he decided to come home to take over as the farm's fifth Bardenhagen.

Fast-forward to 2013. Now it was Jim getting ready to retire.

Will the farm have a sixth generation?

In Northern Michigan, tourists and seasonal residents buy cherry T-shirts and cherry refrigerator magnets. They sip cherry–mocha truffle lattes, have salads spiked with dried cherries, then fly home out of Cherry Capital Airport.

And for a short time each summer, they snack on sweet cherries they pick up at roadside stands. Cherry growers spend about fifty weeks a year tending their cherry trees and two weeks harvesting.

Everything has to happen quickly, because so much can go wrong.

Speed is imperative. The shelf life of a sweet cherry is brief. It's as perfect as it will ever be the minute it comes off the tree.

But that assumes it didn't rain in the days before harvest. If moisture collects on a ripe cherry, it can cause an unsightly scar. It actually sweetens the fruit, but the blemish eliminates it from the fresh cherry market. Those cherries are destined for juice. Or the pigs.

It also assumes the cherries made it through spring. An early warming can trigger production, and then there's no turning back. If there's a freeze after those blooms set—not an uncommon occurrence—it can knock out that season's cherries.

And all that assumes a developer hasn't razed the orchard to build hotels or houses, tearing out the farmland that brings people here in the first place.

These are the kinds of things that Jim has been dealing with since he took over the farm. There isn't much he can do about the weather, but he does what he can to protect farms on

the Leelanau Peninsula, a sliver of land that juts into Lake Michigan.

Tourism and a burgeoning wine industry have driven up the price of land in the area, which has put a lot of pressure on farmers to sell their property. Jim works with the Leelanau Conservancy, which helps farmers by buying "development rights," effectively paying them to keep farming their land and designating the property as farmland.

Thousands of acres have been protected this way.

Cammie Buehler, who runs a catering operation called Epicure in nearby Omena, had Jim grow potatoes on her property for a few summers. She remembers seeing him out in the field on his tractor. She was struck by how happy he looked there, how content.

She calls Jim the patriarch of the agriculture community. He provides institutional knowledge for young farmers when they need information on things like pest management or harvesting.

He isn't just protecting farmland. He's protecting farming.

If Vernon's legacy to the farm is cherries, Jim's is apples. He added the trees in the early 1990s, and apple season starts a few weeks after cherry season ends, so it keeps the work steady.

Jim heard that local schools were having trouble getting students to eat the fruit included with their lunches. Then he heard that schools were buying apples from out of state. There's your problem. Michigan apples taste better, he said, and the kids know it.

He worked with the schools to get local apples in the lunchroom, and the schools say that the kids are eating their apples now.

Vernon had eight possible successors for the farm. Jim has two. Jim's daughter, Ginger Bardenhagen, already lives on the farm, raising pigs and chickens in her spare time.

In college, she majored in German and spent a semester in Germany. After she finished school, she went back to spend a year.

Well, almost a year. She left after cherry harvest one year and had to be back in time for the next. When you're a Bardenhagen, you always come back for cherry season.

Ginger sees how hard her dad works and how much he puts into the community. She respects it immensely. She isn't sure if she can do it.

But there is so much history. Ginger remembers watching her grandfather work the orchards during those summer vacations as a kid. She has tracked the family tree and appreciates the history of this land.

There was soul-searching. Then there was a plan. Ginger and her husband, Ryan, want to take over the apple orchard. Ginger's brother, Chris, will take the tart cherry trees. They have to figure out how to split up the sweet cherries and potatoes, no small issue since those crops bring in much of the farm's revenue. There are still questions as to whether the farm can support two families. The plan is to figure that out.

Ginger is already thinking about what her stamp on the farm might be. She may build a distillery so she and Ryan can make artisanal spirits from the crops they'll grow.

The evolution continues. The sixth generation is on board.

Check back in a quarter-century to see about the seventh.

APPLE FRITTERS

with Cinnamon Chantilly

The fragrance of frying apples in October may be one of the most powerful of all for a guy who grew up in Washington state. These are quick and easy, and your family and friends will swoon majestic upon their very first bite.

MAKES 12 TO 14 FRITTERS

FOR THE BATTER

1 cup cake flour

½ cup cornstarch

1 tablespoon baking powder

1 teaspoon kosher salt

1 cup ice-cold plain seltzer

1 large egg

2 tablespoons extra-virgin olive oil

FOR THE CINNAMON CHANTILLY

2 cups whipping cream

¼ cup confectioners' sugar

2 teaspoons ground cinnamon

FOR THE CINNAMON-SUGAR

2 teaspoons ground cinnamon

1 cup granulated sugar

FOR THE FRITTERS

1 quart peanut oil, for frying

3 Honeycrisp apples, peeled, cored, and cut into ½-inch-thick rings

MAKE THE BATTER

In a bowl, stir together the flour, cornstarch, baking powder, and salt. In a separate bowl, whisk together the seltzer, egg, and oil. Add the liquid to the dry ingredients and whisk until smooth. The batter should be the texture of crepe batter. If too thick, add more water; if too thin, add more flour.

MAKE THE CINNAMON CHANTILLY

Place a metal bowl in the freezer to chill.

Place the cream in the chilled bowl and whip until soft peaks form, then add the confectioners' sugar and the cinnamon and whip for 20 seconds more. Refrigerate until ready to serve.

MAKE THE CINNAMON-SUGAR

In a bowl, combine the cinnamon and granulated sugar. Set aside.

MAKE THE APPLE FRITTERS

Heat the peanut oil in a high-sided pot until it registers 360°F on a deep-fry thermometer.

Dip each apple slice into the batter. Let the excess batter drip off and carefully place the apple slice in the hot oil. Fry 3 to 4 slices at a time until a light golden color. Drain briefly on paper towels and then dredge in the cinnamon-sugar mixture, coating the fried apple slices evenly.

Serve with cinnamon chantilly on the side.

CLASSIC APPLE TART TATIN

I first figured out this classic apple dessert while watching Julia Child with my grandma in the 1970s. The memories of its incredible balance of rich caramel, sweet and tangy apples, and crisp pastry have lingered in the back of my mind during apple season for the rest of my adult life. I served it at Po, my very first restaurant, and I serve it at home at least a couple of times each fall.

SERVES 8

5 medium Crimson Crisp apples, or another tart apple, such as Granny Smith

Juice of ½ lemon

1 cup sugar

8 tablespoons (1 stick) unsalted butter

1 (14-ounce) box frozen puff pastry, thawed but kept chilled

1 cup sour cream or lightly sweetened whipped cream

Peel and core the apples whole, then halve them crosswise to create doughnut-shaped rounds. In a bowl, toss the apple halves gently with the lemon juice and ¼ cup of the sugar. Set aside for 30 minutes in the fridge.

Preheat the oven to 400°F.

In a 12-inch ovenproof skillet, melt the butter over medium heat. Sprinkle in the remaining ¾ cup sugar and swirl it in the pan until it becomes a golden brown caramel, slightly chunky with granules of unmelted sugar, then remove from the heat. Lay the apples in the skillet, arranging 6 rounds on the perimeter and one in the center. Cut the remaining 3 apple rounds into ½-inch pieces and slide them in between the halves to make it a tight configuration.

Return the pan to the stovetop over medium heat and cook the apples in the caramel for 8 to 10 minutes.

Roll out your puff pastry to a 13- to 14-inch piece and trim it to a circle. Remove the skillet from the heat and lay the pastry round over the apples. The caramel will be extremely hot, so do not touch it with bare fingers, but use a spatula to tuck the edges of the pastry around the apples toward the bottom of the pan, to create a lip on the final tart. At this point, it does not need to look perfect, and if the pastry does not fit exactly, do not fret—just make sure that you can patch together a full cover for the apples and that the pastry (pastry quilt, if you will) goes to the edges of the apples and down over that outer edge.

Continued on page 314.

Bake until the pastry is puffed and golden brown, about 20 minutes—darker is better than lighter.

Remove the tart from the oven and let stand for 2 minutes. Place a plate at least 14 inches around over the pan, serving side toward the apples, and quickly and smoothly flip the pan and the plate upside down together to allow the tart to end up on the plate with the pan on top of it. Shake the pan gently to make sure the apples and the pastry have detached from the pan, and carefully lift the pan away. If there are rogue pieces of apple stuck to the pan, gently move them off of the pan and place them in their spot on the pastry crust.

Serve with a dollop of sour cream and eat immediately.

CHERRY- BROWN BUTTER COFFEE CAKE

SERVES 6 TO 8

FOR THE CAKE

2 tablespoons extra-virgin olive oil, for the pan

8 tablespoons (1 stick) unsalted butter, softened

½ cup granulated sugar

½ cup light brown sugar, packed

1 cup plain Greek yogurt

2 large eggs

1 tablespoon pure vanilla extract

2¼ cups all-purpose flour, plus more for the pan

2 teaspoons baking powder

½ teaspoon baking soda

1 teaspoon kosher salt

2 cups frozen tart cherries, thawed in the fridge

FOR THE TOPPING

¼ cup almond flour

½ cup dark brown sugar, packed

½ cup chopped hazelnuts

1 teaspoon ground cinnamon

1 teaspoon freshly grated nutmeg

3 tablespoons salted butter

Confectioners' sugar, for dusting

1 cup plain Greek yogurt, for serving

Browning the butter is the crucial step here—do not be afraid to take it to medium dark brown before removing the butter from the heat in the first step. It should smell like rich hazelnuts when you take it off the stove.

MAKE THE CAKE

Preheat the oven to 325°F. Oil and flour a 9-by-13-inch baking pan.

Place the unsalted butter in a saucepan over medium heat and cook until the foam subsides and the butter starts to look medium-brown at the bottom of the pan, 4 to 5 minutes. Allow to cool, and place in fridge for 10 minutes to set up to the texture of softened butter.

Combine the granulated sugar, light brown sugar, and cooled brown butter in a large bowl. Beat with an electric mixer at medium speed, scraping down the sides of the bowl often, until creamy. Add the yogurt, eggs, and the vanilla; continue beating until well mixed. Reduce the mixer speed to low and add 2 cups of the flour, the baking powder, baking soda, and salt. Beat until well mixed.

Drain the thawed cherries and reserve the liquid. In a medium bowl, mix the thawed cherries and the remaining ¼ cup flour until the cherries are lightly coated, and set aside.

Stir the reserved cherry liquid into the batter and mix through.

Spread half of the batter into the prepared pan. Spoon the cherry mixture over the batter. Spoon the remaining batter over the cherry filling, spreading it carefully to cover the filling completely.

MAKE THE TOPPING

Combine the almond flour, dark brown sugar, hazelnuts, cinnamon, nutmeg, and butter in a food processor. Pulse quickly 5 or 6 times until the mixture has a bread crumb texture. Sprinkle the topping evenly over the cake batter.

Bake the cake for 45 to 50 minutes, until a toothpick inserted into the center of the cake comes out clean and the topping is a dark golden brown. Dust the top with confectioners' sugar and serve with Greek yogurt on the side.

WALNUT-HONEY CAKE

with Almond Frosting

SERVES 6 TO 8

FOR THE CAKE

Butter, for the pan

1 cup walnut pieces

¼ cup honey

2 cups cake flour

1½ teaspoons baking powder

1 teaspoon baking soda

1 teaspoon kosher salt

1 teaspoon ground cinnamon

½ teaspoon ground cloves

16 tablespoons (2 sticks) butter, softened

¾ cup brown sugar, packed

6 large eggs, at room temperature

Zest and juice of 1 orange

1 (8-ounce) container plain Greek yogurt

FOR THE ALMOND FROSTING

1 cup blanched sliced almonds

1 cup sour cream

1 cup cream cheese

1 cup confectioners' sugar

Zest of 1 orange

This cake has supreme texture, and the frosting is a revelation that I borrowed from Carla Hall ("Ohh, Carla, can you let me use this killer frosting recipe?") when she made the best coconut layer cake ever on The Chew.

MAKE THE CAKE

Preheat the oven to 350°F. Butter a 9-by-13-inch metal baking pan.

In a food processor, combine the walnuts with the honey and process until the walnuts are finely ground into a paste.

In a separate bowl, combine the flour, baking powder, baking soda, salt, cinnamon, and cloves.

In the bowl of a stand mixer fitted with the paddle attachment, beat the butter with the brown sugar on medium speed until creamy.

Add the eggs, one at a time, beating well after each addition, then add the orange zest and juice.

With the mixer on low speed, alternately add the flour mixture and the yogurt, beginning and ending with the flour mixture; beat just until the batter is smooth, occasionally scraping down the bowl with a rubber spatula.

Fold in the walnut mixture.

Spread the batter in the prepared pan and bake for 30 to 35 minutes, until a toothpick inserted into the center of the cake comes out clean. Leave the oven on.

Transfer the pan to a wire rack and let the cake cool completely in the pan.

MAKE THE ALMOND FROSTING

While the cake is cooling, toast the almonds in the preheated oven on a dry baking sheet for 6 minutes until very light brown and then let them cool.

Place the sour cream and cream cheese in a bowl and stir until smooth, then stir in the confectioners' sugar and the almonds. Refrigerate, covered, for 30 minutes.

When the cake is cool, frost it, sprinkle with the zest, and refrigerate for 30 minutes.

Cut into 3-inch squares and serve.

CORNMEAL, HONEY, AND RICOTTA FRITTERS

These spectacular fritters take a little work to make, but you can freeze them raw and actually fry them directly out of the freezer, so you can make them up to a month ahead.

MAKES 12 FRITTERS

1 cup cottage cheese

1 cup sheep's milk ricotta

Zest of 2 oranges

2 large eggs

1 cup plain Greek yogurt

¼ cup tupelo honey

1¼ cups superfine cornmeal

1¼ cups superfine semolina

½ cup heavy cream, warmed

8 tablespoons (1 stick) unsalted butter, softened

2 cups extra-virgin olive oil

Confectioners' sugar, for dusting

1 cup bitter honey, such as corbezzolo, warmed

In a bowl, stir together the cottage cheese, ricotta, orange zest, eggs, yogurt, and honey until well blended.

In a separate bowl, mix the cornmeal and semolina and form a well in the center. In a small saucepan, stir together the warmed cream and butter until the butter has melted. Pour the cream mixture into the well in the flour mixture and incorporate wet into dry to form a dough. Knead the dough for 1 minute, form into a ball, wrap, and refrigerate for 1 hour.

Heat the oil in a high-sided pan until it registers 375°F on a deep-fry thermometer.

With a pasta roller, roll out the pastry to ¼-inch thickness. Cut twenty-six 3-inch rounds out of the pastry. Place 2 tablespoons of the cheese mixture on 13 of the rounds and cover each like a sandwich with another round of dough. Press the edges together to seal and press down around the edges with the tines of a fork. Place on a tray and refrigerate for 10 minutes.

Gently drop the fritters into the hot oil and fry until golden brown, about 1 minute. Using a slotted spoon or spider, transfer the fritters to paper towels to drain.

Dust with confectioners' sugar and serve with warm bitter honey.

Note that the yield for this recipe is 12 fritters, but it makes 13. Eat one before they go to the table. You deserve it.

THE CHEFS AND THE FARMERS

Austin

THE CHEF   BRYCE GILMORE is the executive chef and owner of Barley Swine and Odd Duck in Austin, Texas. He was named one of *Food & Wine* magazine's Best New Chefs in 2011, and GQ included Barley Swine on its list of best new restaurants in 2012. www.barleyswine.com

THE FARMER   NATHAN HEATH is the owner and farmer at Phoenix Farms in Bastrop, Texas, where he works with his wife, Shayda, and his mother, Cindy. He recently started a program to help teach farming to people who are considering the field. www.phoenixfarmstx.com

Chicago

THE CHEF   PAUL KAHAN has earned international acclaim for his Chicago restaurants, including The Publican, Blackbird, Avec, and Nico Osteria. He won the James Beard Foundation's Outstanding Chef award in 2013 and was a *Food & Wine* Best New Chef in 1999, but considers mentoring young chefs his biggest accomplishment. www.oneoffhospitality.com

THE FARMER   DAVID CLEVERDON is the owner and farmer at Kinnikinnick Farm in Caledonia, Illinois, and a member of the board of Chicago's Greencity Market and the Frontera Farmer Foundation. www.kinnikinnickfarm.com

Cleveland

THE CHEF   MICHAEL SYMON is the chef/owner of restaurants in Cleveland and Detroit. He is a host of ABC's *The Chew* and has appeared on several Food Network shows. He was one of *Food & Wine* magazine's Best New Chefs in 1998 and James Beard's Best Chef: Great Lakes in 2009. www.lolitarestaurant.com

THE FARMER   MAGGIE FITZPATRICK is the farm manager at Refugee Response on the Ohio City Farm in Cleveland, Ohio, where she helps educate and train refugees resettling in the Cleveland area. www.refugeeresponse.com

Las Vegas

THE CHEF   DOUG TAYLOR ran the pastry program at Carnevino, B&B Ristorante, and Otto Pizzeria in Las Vegas. He cofounded one of the first farmers' markets in Las Vegas, Bet on the Farm. www.bandbristorante.com

THE FARMER   JON CHODACKI is the orchard manager at the University of Nevada Cooperative Extension Orchard in North Las Vegas. His research includes studying efficient ways to grow crops in the Southern Nevada desert. www.unce.unr.edu/counties/clark

Los Angeles

THE CHEF   MATT MOLINA is the executive chef at Osteria Mozza and Pizzeria Mozza in Los Angeles. In 2012, he won the James Beard Foundation award for Best Chef: Pacific.
www.osteriamozza.com

THE FARMER   ALEX WEISER is a farmer at the family-owned Weiser Family Farms based in Tehachapi, California, where the farms host events to benefit organizations such as the children's cancer charity Alex's Lemonade Stand.
www.weiserfamilyfarms.com

Nashville

THE CHEF   ERIK ANDERSON was the executive chef of The Catbird Seat in Nashville, Tennessee. In 2012, he was named one of *Food & Wine* magazine's Best New Chefs, and The Catbird Seat was named one of the country's best new restaurants by *Bon Appétit* and *GQ*.
www.thecatbirdseatrestaurant.com

THE FARMER   KAREN OVERTON is a fourth-generation farmer at Wedge Oak Farm in Lebanon, Tennessee. She sells chicken, duck, eggs, and pork to restaurants and at farmers' markets in and around Nashville.
www.wedgeoakfarm.com

New York City

THE CHEF   DAN DROHAN has been cooking in Italian restaurants since he was fourteen and was hired at Otto Enoteca and Pizzeria in New York City in 2004. He has been the executive chef there since 2005.
www.ottopizzeria.com

THE FARMER   TIM STARK is the owner and farmer at Eckerton Hill Farm in Lobachsville, Pennsylvania, two hours west of New York City. He sells his tomatoes and vegetables to restaurants in the city, and at the Union Square Greenmarket.
www.eckertonhillfarm.com

Rockland, Maine

THE CHEF   MELISSA KELLY is the chef/owner of Primo Restaurant in Rockland, Maine, which *Bon Appétit* named one of its 20 Most Important Restaurants in America in 2013. The restaurant also has locations in Orlando and Tucson. She won the James Beard Foundation award for Best Chef: Northeast in 1999 and 2013.
www.primorestaurant.com

THE FARMER   JEFF "SMOKEY" MCKEEN farms oysters on the Damariscotta River in Maine with his partners in Pemaquid Oyster Company. With his band Old Grey Goose, he tours the world playing traditional music of the region. Each September, he helps host an oyster festival in Damariscotta.
www.pemaquidoysters.com

San Francisco

THE CHEF   BRUCE HILL is the chef/partner of several San Francisco–area restaurants, including Picco, Fog City, Bix, and Zero Zero. In 1997, he was named a Rising Star Chef by *Wine Spectator* magazine.
www.fogcitysf.com

THE FARMER   ANDY GRIFFIN is the owner and farmer at Mariquita Farm, based in Watsonville, California. Mariquita serves about fifty restaurants in the San Francisco area and area families through a community-sponsored agriculture program.
www.mariquita.com

Seattle

THE CHEF   MATT DILLON is the chef/owner of several restaurants in Seattle, Washington, including Sitka & Spruce, The Corson Building, and Bar Sajor. He won the James Beard Foundation's Best Chef: Northwest award in 2012 and was one of *Food & Wine* magazine's Best New Chefs in 2007.
www.sitkaandspruce.com

THE FARMER   PIERRE MONNAT is the farmer at Old Chaser Farm on Vashon Island, Washington, where he raises vegetables and livestock for a community-sponsored agriculture program. He also shears sheep across Washington.
www.oldchaserfarm.com

Suttons Bay, Michigan

THE CHEF   CAMMIE BUEHLER is the managing partner and co-owner of Epicure Catering in Omena, Michigan, with chef/co-owner Andy Schudlich. Events and menus designed by Cammie and Andy celebrate the food and farmers of Northern Michigan.
www.caterleelanau.com

THE FARMER   JIM BARDENHAGEN is the owner and farmer at Bardenhagen Farms in Suttons Bay, Michigan, where he grows apples, sweet and tart cherries, and potatoes. He is the fifth generation of the family to farm the land.
www.bardenhagenfarms.com

Tampa

THE CHEF   GREG BAKER is the chef and co-owner of The Refinery and Fodder & Shine in Tampa, Florida. He's a frequent James Beard Foundation nominee, and his menu incorporates classic technique with nearly lost Florida ingredients, which he aims to resurrect.
www.thetamparefinery.com

THE FARMER   REBECCA KRASSNOSKI is the owner of Nature Delivered Farm near Tampa, Florida. She is a minimalist farmer who lives in a tiny, off-grid house utilizing passive systems, repurposed materials, and other sustainable methods to economically raise pigs for restaurants.
www.naturedeliveredfarm.com

Vail, Colorado

THE CHEF KELLY LIKEN's "live in season" tenet inspires her work as the chef/owner of Restaurant Kelly Liken in Vail, Colorado. She is a frequent James Beard Foundation nominee and has appeared on *Iron Chef America* and *Top Chef*.

www.kellyliken.com

THE FARMER THE VAIL FARMERS MARKET is open on Sundays from June to October. Vendors include Miller Farms, a family farm in Platteville since 1949; Jumpin' Good Goat Dairy, a cheesemaker in Buena Vista; Eat a Peach, a farm based in Palisade; and Ripe, which sells produce from farmers around the state.

www.millerfarms.net / www.jumpingoodgoats.com

Washington, D.C.

THE CHEF JOSÉ ANDRÉS is the chef/owner of more than a dozen restaurants in locations from Los Angeles to Washington, D.C., and is a noted food advocate/philanthropist. In 2012, he won the James Beard Foundation's Outstanding Chef award and was named to *Time* magazine's list of 100 Most Influential People.

www.joseandres.com

THE FARMER JIM CRAWFORD is the owner and farmer at New Morning Farm in Hustontown, Pennsylvania. He helped start the Tuscarora Organic Growers Cooperative, which organizes the distribution of crops from about fifty farmers in central Pennsylvania to the Washington, D.C., area.

www.newmorningfarm.net

INDEX

*of recipes by the city
that inspired them*

Acknowledgments
FROM MARIO

Without my team, I am nothing.

Susi, Benno, and Leo, who make life the constant source of joy that it is.

My communications team led by Pamela Murphy, with David Gruber, Katy-Jo Previte, and Tess Koenig, for making everything work smoothly with aplomb, poise, and style.

Designer Douglas Riccardi and his team at Memo for making the pages smart and beautiful.

Photo shoot art director, food artist Krista Ruane.

Chef and kitchen manager Liz Benno and her team, Verinder Carouse and Justin Skribner.

Prop stylist Rick Gilbert, for truly being the coolest prop person on this planet.

My editor Karen Murgolo at Grand Central Life & Style, for making this a smooth and delightful process. And kudos to her team, Matthew Ballast in publicity, Pippa White, Morgan Hedden, and Kallie Shimek in editorial.

Food photographer Quentin Bacon for his brilliance on the page and in the kitchen studio.

Still photographer Kelly Campbell for her patience and happiness in poultry.

My business partners Joe Bastianich, Lidia Bastianich, John Farber, the Farinetti and Saper clans, and Mary Giuliani for thinking big. Plus Tom Zidian and the team at Summer Garden Foods and the teams at Madeira Housewares and Dansk.

The hardworking teams at my restaurants and grocery stores for exceeding all expectations and understanding the importance of our collaboration; and more importantly, their families, for tolerating the amount of hard work we all put into our days, every day.

Cathy Frankel for keeping it all under one roof and consistent.

Tony Gardner for persevering in the truly intense and silly grind that contracts have become in a way that always impresses me.

Susan Marzano at my foundation for working hard to raise money to help share our joy.

Reyna Mastrosimone for constantly keeping the digital and entertainment world near.

To *The Chew* crew—Dafo, Symon, Clinton, and Carla—for making every day at work fun and funny at the same time.

To Jim Harrison, Izzy, and Gabe for the voices in my head reminding me again to love the day and the night, every day, every night…

Thanks to...

Pam Webster, for being my sounding board and an incredible in-house editor, and for feeding the cats.

My colleagues at the *Washington Post*—including Joe Yonan, Bonnie Benwick, Courtney Rukan, Jesse Lewis, and Tracy Grant—for setting the bar high and for giving me the time I needed when I had to drop everything to, say, go to an oyster festival.

Members of Team Mario—including Pamela Murphy, David Gruber, Cathy Frankel, Krista Ruane, Susan Marzano, and Tony Gardner—for making it easy for me to do things I might have thought impossible.

Photographers Lara Cerri and Christine Birch Ferrelli for helping me figure it out as we went along.

All the chefs' assistants and representatives who facilitated access, including Heather Medina, Rebecca Yody, Sarah Johns, Vanessa Kanegai, Ali Slutsky, Ann McCarthy, and Russell Bermel.

Michelle and Greg Baker, for hosting some of the key conversations that led to this book.

Friends who listened, encouraged, and/or offered logistical help, including Becky and Jeremy Bowers, Melanie Starkey and Josh Korr, Carrie Alexander and Barry Harrell, Pam and Jim Radabaugh, Ronnie Perkins, Laura Reiley, Carol Blymire, Heidi Robb, Tony Ferrelli, Ted McLaren, Suzy Mast Lee, Alison Steele, and Darcie Purcell.

And Tammy James, for continued inspiration.

Acknowledgments
FROM JIM

INDEX

PHOTOGRAPHY CREDITS

The photographs on the following pages are by Lara Cerri: 2, 6, 11–13, 32–35, 162–163, 178–181, 202–205, 315, 322-323, 326 (Nashville), 329 (Tampa), 330 (Washington, D.C.), 331, 336, 348, 352.

The photographs on the following pages are by Christine Birch Ferrelli: 20–23, 42–43, 48, 54–57, 66–67, 76–79, 85, 96–99, 108–109, 116–119, 136–139, 150–153, 227, 234–235, 246–249, 262–265, 273, 276–277, 288–291, 306*, 308–309, 324, 325**, 326 (Los Angeles), 327***, 328, 329 (Suttons Bay), 330 (Vail), 338.

The photographs on pages 8 and 350 are by Kelly Campbell.

The photograph on pages 128–129 is by Kate Previte.

The photograph on page 351 is by Deb Lindsey.

*The photograph of cherry crates on page 306 is by Jim Webster.

**The photograph of Michael Symon on page 325 is courtesy of Michael Symon Restaurants.

***The photograph of Melissa Kelly on page 327 is by Pam Webster.

ABOUT THE AUTHORS

Mario Batali counts among his accomplishments twenty-six restaurants around the globe, nine cookbooks, numerous television shows, and two Eataly marketplaces in New York and Chicago. Batali's cookbooks include the James Beard Award–winning *Molto Italiano: 327 Simple Italian Recipes* and *Molto Batali: Simple Family Meals from My Home to Yours*. Batali appears daily on ABC's *The Chew*, a daytime talk show that celebrates and explores life through food. In 2008, he founded the Mario Batali Foundation with the mission of feeding, protecting, educating, and empowering children.

Jim Webster is a newspaperman by trade and a culinary adventurer by choice. When not at his job at the *Washington Post*, he can be found in the kitchen, at the farmers' market, or out learning from the chefs and farmers who feed us all so he can produce more delicious content.